Introducing MACROBIOTIC COOKING

Introducing

Macrobiotic Cooking

by **Wendy Esko**

with a Foreword by Aveline Kushi
illustrations by Bonnie Harris

JAPAN PUBLICATIONS, INC.

Japan Publications Edition

Copyright © 1978 by Wendy Esko

This book was originally published under the title of *An Introduction to Macrobiotic Cooking* by East West Foundation, 17 Station Street, Brookline, Massachusetts 02147. This Japan Publications Edition is published by arrangement with East West Foundation.

Published by JAPAN PUBLICATIONS, INC., Tokyo • New York

Distributors:
UNITED STATES: *Kodansha International/USA, Ltd., through Harper & Row, Publishers, Inc., 10 East 53rd Street, New York, New York 10022.* SOUTH AMERICA: *Harper & Row, Publishers, Inc., International Department.* CANADA: *Fitzhenry & Whiteside Ltd., 150 Lesmill Road, Don Mills, Ontario M3B 2T6.* MEXICO AND CENTRAL AMERICA: *HARLA S. A. de C. V., Apartado 30–546, Mexico 4, D. F.* BRITISH ISLES: *International Book Distributors Ltd., 66 Wood Lane End, Hemel Hempstead, Herts HP2 4RG.* EUROPEAN CONTINENT: *Fleetbooks, S. A., c/o Feffer and Simons (Nederland) B. V., Rijnkade 170, 1382 GT Weesp, The Netherlands.* AUSTRALIA AND NEW ZEALAND: *Bookwise, 1 Jeanes Street, Beverley, South Australia 5009.* THE FAR EAST AND JAPAN: *Japan Publications Trading Co., Ltd., 1–2–1, Sarugaku-cho, Chiyoda-ku, Tokyo 101.*

First edition: September 1979
Eleventh printing: July 1984

LCCC No. 79–1957
ISBN 0–87040–458–x

Printed in U.S.A.

Foreword

Professor Harvey Cox, of the Harvard Divinity School, mentioned to my husband and I over lunch one day at the Seventh Inn that students who eat during his field trips are more alert and seem to remember more than those who attend trips during which no meals are served. It was an interesting observation because the macrobiotic way of life is intimately related to our daily food and its influence on every aspect of our lives.

Many people, when they first hear about macrobiotics, do not understand or agree with its approach to life. It seems to me, however, that they cannot easily forget the simple truth that we create our physical, mental and spiritual condition by the foods we eat.

Since living in Boston we have always had two or three people staying in our home, for the purpose of studying macrobiotics. At first, not satisfied with other people's cooking, I prepared all the food myself. But as time passed, I came to enjoy the young students' cooking. Some students have stayed with us for six months or a year, living just like members of the family. It has been very enjoyable to see the improvement in their way of cooking and in their health. Many have become excellent cooks and many now have beautiful families.

One day, our Japanese friend, Mr. Matsui, saw a young lady cooking a macrobiotic meal in our home and asked, "She is *uchideshi?*" *Uchideshi* means to live and study in the traditional way. Mr. Matsui, who is a Noh Drama professional, studied in this ancient manner, living in his master's house and training very strictly, for nearly 20 years.

In Japan, many traditional arts and crafts, such as swordmaking, carpentry, tea ceremony and restaurant cooking are learned by living and training in the master's or teacher's home. From a young age, I have heard how strict these teachers are and how difficult it is to study in this manner.

We did not adopt the disciplinarian ways of traditional Japanese teaching in our home. The students living with us are considered family members who are learning to apply the principles of macrobiotics in their daily lives.

Wendy Esko and her husband, Edward, lived with us for almost three years. Wendy was very busy helping to establish the East West Foundation and doing related work and did not have much time to cook. But, after she moved into her own home, she began cooking regularly, teaching cooking classes and helping many people learn and adopt the macrobiotic way of life.

From time to time I meet her shopping in the Erewhon food store. To fill the needs of her family and the students in her home, she buys a wide variety of macrobiotic groceries and I often tease her, saying, "Seems that you are having another party!"

I understand how the energy of the food Wendy has eaten has been changed into her cookbook. I am very happy to see this basic, yet comprehensive guide. The recipes and advice that follow will enable many people to learn the principles of macrobiotic cooking and will help them to establish their own and their families' health and happiness.

Rather than being a fixed or limited regime, eating macrobiotically is as flexible and varied as the natural world itself. It actually offers more variety than the standard fare and, as you will see, the preparation and way of eating, when done properly, can become an expression of art in our daily lives.

The study of cooking is endless and we should continually strive to refine our technique in accordance with the ever-changing circumstances of our lives. I encourage all macrobiotic people to try new recipes and to experiment with the different ways of preparation, but please do not forget to study the real principle of macrobiotics.

This book is very good for beginning basic macrobiotic cooking. I hope you can further your spiritual development with your practice of cooking. Once you begin to discover the value of the macrobiotic way of cooking, please encourage and help others.

I would like to thank Wendy once again for her efforts in creating such a practical and informative cookbook.

AVELINE KUSHI
Brookline, Massachusetts
June, 1978

Preface

It is remarkable how the most important things in our lives are often so obvious that they either go unrecognized or are barely noticed at all. Such is the case with our daily acts of cooking and eating.

Cooking is the art of creating life itself. From it arises all of our happinesses and unhappiness, successes and failures, our health or sickness, our longevity or premature death. The quality of our diet determines whether our life is one of continuing health and development, or one of progressive decline and decay. Cooking is so vital that every person, both male and female, should have a good working knowledge of how to select and prepare basic daily foods. This education should begin at home as soon as a child is able to speak, and should continue throughout life. Proper cooking is essential to every aspect of our life and future destiny, yet we rarely find a school or college which even includes basic cooking instruction in its curriculum.

Our modern world is facing grave difficulties brought on entirely as a result of our ignoring the importance of food and cooking. One need only refer to the statistics which record the epidemic increases in cancer, heart disease, stroke, mental illness, and other degenerative illnesses, as well as social decline and disorder, to confirm just how widespread are the challenges that confront us as individuals and as a society. As large as these problems seem and as diverse and illusive as their solutions appear to be, each can be traced back to what takes place in the kitchen. A peaceful and healthy world will not be born at conference tables, in scientific laboratories, in college or university seminars, or through international negotiations or discussions. It will emerge as we come to understand the importance of food and begin to apply it in our daily lives. In a very real sense, we can say that a peaceful and happy world begins in the kitchen.

In the midst of this physical and social decay that confronts us, however, is the growing awareness that proper food and proper cooking is the way of reversing our modern, unhealthy and unhappy predicament. From the steadily expanding natural foods movement, to the emerging interest among leaders in government and medicine, we see the growth of a realistic attitude toward food and its relationship to our complete well being.

It is inevitable that the majority of people in the United States and other modern nations will eventually shift toward a more ecological and natural diet. However, the substitution of organic for chemicalized products or the inclusion of a few natural items into the daily menu will not automatically produce the necessary conditions for the development of health and well being. What we need is a comprehensive understanding of the proper way to select, prepare, serve, and consume our daily food.

Since our life depends on food, we must not accept anything less than dietary principles which are based on the order of nature and the universe itself. It is just these principles that the macrobiotic way of cooking and eating has to offer, not only to those involved in the natural foods movement, but to every human being. Through these basic universal principles we can understand what the proper food for man is under any conditions, and know how to create our evolutionary destiny. It is our hope that those people searching for a more natural way of eating and living will use these principles as the basis for establishing their health.

Macrobiotic cooking is based on achieving and maintaining a balance with our natural environment. The origin of this balance is the two fundamental tendencies which are found throughout the universe and which govern all phenomena. In macrobiotics, we refer to these universal tendencies as yin and yang.

Yin represents the primary expansion of the infinite universe itself, and produces such relative manifestations as centrifugality, expansion, low temperature, upward growth or motion, the female sex, diffusion, lightness, and countless other appearances. Yang represents the primary force of condensation or materialization which arises within the infinite depth of the universe. It produces such relative appearances as centripetal force or movement, contraction, high temperature, downward growth or motion, the male sex, density, heaviness, and countless other appearances.

In macrobiotic cooking, we apply the various yin and yang factors in our food and environment to create balanced meals. The more yang environmental factors include fire, pressure, salt, and time (aging); while the more yin factors are oil, water, lack of pressure, and less cooking time (freshness). Foods, like every phenomena in the universe, can be classified into these two general categories, the more yin vegetable quality foods and the more yang animal quality foods. Also, within each category, individual items can be identified as more yin or more yang.

Cooking, for the most part, is the process whereby we take more yin, vegetable-quality foods and yangize them with fire, pressure, salt, aging, and other factors to varying degrees, in order to balance our natural and social environments. In all but the most extreme polar climates, the mainstay of our diet should be vegetable-quality foods. However, when we do use animal foods, it is possible to make them more yin with the appropriate cooking techniques.

Proceeding along the scale from yang to yin, daily food items can be classified as follows: salt, eggs, meat, poultry, fish, more yang grains like buckwheat, rice and other more balanced grains, corn, more yang beans such as *azuki*, chickpea, and lentil, root vegetables such as burdock and carrots, ground vegetables like squash and cabbage, sea vegetables, various green leafy vegetables like watercress, *daikon* and carrot greens, parsley, and others, seeds and nuts, temperate climate fruits such as apples, strawberries, and cherries, tropical fruits such as oranges, grapefruit, bananas, and pineapple, concentrated sweeteners such as honey, maple syrup, and molasses, refined sugar, chemical additives, and drugs and medications. Among dairy foods, hard, salty cheeses would be classified as more yang; while milk, yogurt, cottage cheese, and butter are usually more yin.

In order to create the ideal condition for continuing health and adaptability, it is necessary to choose foods which are relatively near the center of the yin—yang scale. The most ideal ratio between yin and yang factors in our daily food is about seven to one (5:1 to 10:1). Among the possible daily food items, whole cereal grains most closely approximate this ratio, and it is for this reason that they should comprise the principal food in the human diet.

Locally grown, seasonal vegetables should comprise the main secondary food, followed by beans, sea vegetables, some animal food, preferably in the form of fish, locally grown seasonal fruits, seeds and nuts, and other occasional supplements. Foods from either extreme of the scale, such as more yang foods like meat and animal products, and more yin items such as sugar, tropical fruits, and drugs and medications, will produce an excessive or unbalanced condition within the body, leading eventually to illnesses of various types.

For this reason such extremes are generally avoided in the practice of macrobiotics. Please refer to the guidelines in Appendix A, "The Standard Macrobiotic Way of Eating," for the recommended proportions of suitable food items, along with a more complete list of foods to be avoided for the development of health in a temperate climate. We can summarize the principles of macrobiotics as follows:

1. *We should eat according to human tradition.* Until recently, the majority of the world's population based their diet around whole grains and local vegetables. With very few exceptions, this trend was universal—appearing in the dietary customs of people in both East and West. In fact, we can trace the use of cereal grains as a principal food back to the origins of the human species itself. Animal products, including dairy foods, were used much less frequently than at present, generally under unusual circumstances.
2. *We should vary our diet according to climate.* The diet of someone living in Brazil obviously should differ from that of someone living in Montreal. More yin, northern climates require the selection of slightly more yang food items along with emphasis on more yang factors in cooking, while balance is maintained in a more yang, tropical climate through the selection of more yin food items, with the use of less salt, pressure, fire, and other more yang factors. We violate the natural ecological order of eating when we begin to include items in our diet which have come from climates which differ from our own. Therefore, people living in temperate climates should avoid, whenever possible, the use of bananas, pineapples, citrus fruits, coffee, spices, and other products which originate in the tropics. It is

possible, however, to maintain our health by importing high quality food items which have grown in climates similar to those in which we live, although, ideally, our diet should consist of foods grown in the same environment.

3. *Our diet should vary with the changing seasons.* Today, most people eat a relatively uniform diet throughout the year. For example, ice cream and cold soft drinks are often consumed throughout the winter, while eggs, meat, and other animal products are frequently consumed during the heat of the summer. Naturally, a diet of this type permits very little adaptation to the changing seasons. In macrobiotics, we try to harmonize our condition with these seasonal changes by emphasizing more yang foods and cooking methods during the cold winter months and by serving more yin, fresh and lightly cooked foods during the summer.

   As much as possible, we should try to base our diet on foods which are naturally available in our area during a particular season, or which can be stored without the artificial methods of freezing, canning, or chemical preservation. Cereal grains, beans, sea vegetables, fermented foods such as *miso*, *tamari*, and pickles, and other foods which can be naturally stored in a cool dry place throughout the year, should comprise the majority of our diet.

4. *Our diet should vary according to personal need.* Since everyone is unique, no two people should or ever can eat the same diet. Every person has different needs based on such variables as age, sex, season of birth, previous eating habits, physical condition, type of activity, and others. All of these must be taken into account when we select and prepare our daily food.

5. *Our food should have a delicious taste and a beautiful and natural appearance.* Through macrobiotics, we can easily maintain our physical, mental and spiritual health. However, health is not the final goal of macrobiotics, but only a means to the enjoyment of life. Simple, natural, whole foods, when properly prepared and aesthetically served, are actually the most appealing to our taste. We should not have the feeling that we are denying ourselves any particular taste or range of foods, but should understand that through macrobiotics, our appreciation of tastes expands tremendously. Our food should at all times be delicious and appealing and we should thoroughly enjoy it. If this is not the case, or if we feel we are missing something in our daily meals, our application is incomplete. At this time we should strive to refine our cooking techniques.

As you can see, the macrobiotic way of eating is not a certain fixed regime, and cannot be called a diet. It is based on flexible adaptation to our ever-changing environment.

In the beginning, the macrobiotic principle—yin and yang—may seem strange or difficult to apply. However, keep in mind that no matter what you are eating, you are always balancing these two complementary and antagonistic factors in your diet as well as in every aspect of life. If, for example, you take too much salt, you will instinctively be drawn to liquid, sugar or other yin foods. This intuitive capacity develops even before birth and continues throughout life. Macrobiotics is nothing but the refinement of this intuition through the conscious application of the order of the universe or yin and yang.

Once you are able to use natural and healthful ingredients to create attractive and delicious meals, you will begin to see that you are not following any particular diet but instead are simply eating in the way a human being was intended to. At the same time, you will begin to realize that proper food is the key to a healthy, free, and happy life—the secret which has been in front of us all along.

EDWARD ESKO
Brookline, Massachusetts
June, 1978

Acknowledgments

I would like to take this opportunity to thank Michio and Aveline Kushi for their constant teaching, inspiration, guidance and support. Through their example and teachings, they have given me and all of their students an understanding of the order of the universe and the key which enables us to create our own health and happiness. I would also like to extend my special thanks to Mrs. Kushi for writing the foreword to this book.

I would also like to thank Edward and Elizabeth Esko, along with Mrs. Edith Kalan and Marge Webster, for making the printing of the book possible, and for their inspiration, guidance, and support.

I thank my ancestors and parents for making it possible for me to be here to write this book, thus helping others find health and happiness.

For his patience, constant inspiration, encouragement and guidance, I give special thanks to my husband, Edward.

To Bonnie and Peter Harris, who illustrated and designed this book, I am very grateful. This project has involved a great deal of work and many long hours. Thank you very much.

I would like to express my gratitude to Phillip Jannetta for doing the editing and final proofreading of the manuscript. I also thank him for being the first person to try out these recipes as he was editing the book, and offering his comments.

I would like to thank Olivia Oredson for the many long hours she has spent typing the manuscript, and I extend my appreciation for her constant support, inspiration and guidance.

I would also like to thank Stephen and Tamra Uprichard, Caroline Heidenry, Yoko Kendall, Isabel Mann, Caludie Belizaire, Terry Schaffer, Linda MaGosse, Sachiko Shimooka, and many others for their comments, guidance, and inspiration.

To all the others, too numerous to mention, who I have studied with, talked to, taught and learned from, thank you.

Finally, I would like to thank all of my students who have been patiently awaiting the printing of this book. I sincerely hope that, in some small way, it will help you establish your own health and happiness, and that you will begin to share your understanding with others, so that the creation of one peaceful world will come about in our life-time.

—W.E.

Contents

Introduction

Nearly seven years ago, I noticed a sign in a natural food store owned by a friend in my home town in upstate New York. The sign was an announcement for a series of natural foods cooking classes.

I had always loved to cook, so I decided to attend the class in order to learn some new recipes. I had no conscious desire to drastically change my diet and no indication of the adventure I was about to set out on. The class was divided into two parts: the first was a discussion of yin and yang and the philosophy of macrobiotics, and the second was a cooking demonstration. I was so confused at first about these two new words—yin and yang—and all that they implied, that I really didn't hear much of the lecture. What I did hear, however, was interesting enough to keep me there.

After the cooking class, everyone had the opportunity to taste the meal which had been prepared. The very first thing that I noticed about the food was its pure and clean taste, which was unlike anything I had ever tasted before. Of course, the food was different from what I had been eating, and some items, such as the seaweed and *miso*, were a little strange, but I couldn't forget how wholesome it was and how good it felt to eat. This impression was so strong that I knew then and there that I wanted to change my eating habits.

That evening, after class, I went home and cleaned my cupboards and refrigerator of all canned and packaged foods, sugar, dairy, animal food, etc. The following day, I went to the natural food store and bought brown rice and other grains, beans, seaweeds, *miso*, *tamari*, fresh vegetables, and other whole foods, and completely restocked my kitchen. That evening I prepared my first macrobiotic meal. Having no idea of how much of this new food to cook, I ended up eating millet soup, *hijiki*, brown rice, and pinto beans for several days.

Of course I did many things wrong in those beginning years, but I always learned by my mistakes. I cooked with too much salt and became too yang. Then I would eat too much yin and end up getting sick. But gradually I learned the meaning of balance and how to judge and use yin and yang.

As I had no books about macrobiotics and only one cookbook by George Ohsawa, I knew nothing about the healing properties of the macrobiotic way of eating. However, as I continued to cook and eat in this way, I noticed that I began to feel so healthy and strong. As I attended more cooking classes and became good friends with my cooking teacher, I began to understand the infinite applicability of macrobiotics.

As I changed my diet, many of my friends began coming to dinner and asking how I prepared the food. Several nights a week, I would cook for about ten people at my home.

In 1973 I moved into a macrobiotic study house in Philadelphia managed by my good friends Denny and Judy Waxman. It was there that I learned of the teaching of Michio and Aveline Kushi in Boston. I knew then that I would someday to go there to study. I met my husband, Edward, in Philadelphia and I soon decided to move to Boston. I began studying with Michio and Aveline Kushi, while at the same time working at the East West Foundation. It was at this time that I had the good fortune to live in the Kushis' home. I am deeply grateful for having had this opportunity It provided me with the chance to experience the cooking of Mrs. Kushi and of the many other women who cooked in the Kushis' home during the several years that I lived there.

It is a great responsibility to cook for twenty people or even for one other person. By cooking for them, you are creating their mental, physical, and spiritual condition, and their biological destiny. A cook should be sensitive to each person's individual needs. In many ways, the kitchen is like a shrine or a temple where you, the cook or creator, are directing the health and happiness of your family and therefore of mankind.

The aim of macrobiotic cooking is to achieve balance or harmony, both within ourselves and with our surrounding environment. If our cooking is balanced, all those who eat it will achieve a balanced condition through which they are able to work, study, play, or do whatever they desire in an efficient way without becoming sick as a result of being overly yin or overly yang. As we achieve balance within ourselves, our relationship with family, friends, and society will become harmonious. When we enter the kitchen, we should strive to develop a feeling of love and respect for nature, the food that we are preparing, for society, and for the people who will eat our cooking.

I have been teaching formal cooking classes for the short period of two years. Teaching is a great challenge and experience, and every time I give a class I learn something new. During each class I am often asked questions which inspire me to think, study, experience, create, and grow. I have also found it very helpful to have several girls living in my home, whom I privately instruct on a daily basis.

This simple, introductory book is based on what I have learned from cooking and studying with Aveline Kushi and other women, from teaching public and private cooking classes, and from cooking for my family and friends.

Experience has taught me that it is helpful at first to imitate the recipes that you learn in class or that you find in cookbooks, at least until you become familiar with the use of a variety of foods as well as the art of balancing the yin and yang factors in your meals. As your condition improves, you will find that you no longer have to rely upon recipes and will begin to create your own cooking style. At that time, you can use cookbooks or classes as sources of new ideas.

Macrobiotics is not just a way of cooking, but is a total way of life. Learning to cook macrobiotically is an endless study. The more you understand, the more you realize that there is no end to the learning process. With health and humility, life can remain an adventure no matter how old we grow. I hope that through studying and using some of the recipes contained in this book, you will gain the ability to achieve your own health and happines, and that you will soon begin to create your own style of cooking.

I would like to express my deepest gratitude to Michio and Aveline Kushi for their guidance, support, and friendship; to George and Lima Ohsawa, for introducing macrobiotics throughout the world and for dedicating their lives to spreading this teaching; to all of the other people I have studied with; and to my friends and family for their constant support, guidance, and inspiration. I would also like to thank all of the people who have attended my cooking classes for providing me with the chance to learn and grow with them. I also thank all of you who read this book for giving me the opportunity to write it. Preparing the book has been a learning experience which has influenced my entire life.

WENDY ESKO
Brookline, Massachusetts
April, 1978

Preparation for Cooking

Cooking Utensils

As you begin cooking macrobiotically, you may gradually need to purchase new utensils that will enable you to prepare foods more efficiently and naturally. The following suggestions are designed to help you choose high-quality kitchenware.

Avoid using aluminum or teflon pots and utensils whenever possible. Aluminum is easily scratched and tends to oxidize, leaving traces of the metal in your food. Aluminum draws radiation from the air, thus raising the temperature of foods, causing them to spoil quickly. It destroys the taste and the life of your food. Teflon also scratches easily and there is the danger of the chemical it is treated with getting into your food.

I have found that heavy pots, pans, and skillets, such as those made of cast-iron or enameled cast-iron, are the best for daily use. They distribute heat evenly, require a lower temperature, use less water in cooking and are easy to clean. A simple soaking in warm water followed by a sponge wash is usually all that is required. Metal cleaning pads will scratch enameled cast-iron, and eventually wear through the enamel coating, causing it to crack and chip. I suggest that you do not use them.

Cast-iron skillets need to be seasoned before use to remove the iron taste. Do this by first roasting salt in the pan, then, after removing the salt, brush the inside heavily with oil and sauté an onion in it. Remove the onion and bake the pan in the oven for several hours at 250–350 degrees F. After seasoning, avoid roasting salt in your pans, as it will destroy the coating and cause them to rust. To prevent rusting, dry your cast-iron skillet thoroughly and then place it over a low flame for several minutes to evaporate any remaining moisture. If your skillet is well-seasoned, it is not necessary to place it on a flame. Simply dry it very well with a towel. Immersing a hot skillet in water will eventually cause the iron to pit. Always allow the pan to cool first before washing.

Electric skillets and cooking pots disturb the natural *ki* or life force in your food, thus creating a chaotic vibration. Avoid them when possible.

I also recommend using stainless steel pots and pans, particularly those with heavy bottoms. Stainless steel heats quickly, thus requiring a fairly low flame, and they clean quite easily.

A pressure-cooker is an essential item in macrobiotic cooking, especially for preparing rice. There are many different kinds of pressure-cookers available, but, for its safety features, I recommend one that has a screw-type pressure gauge. The gauge acts as a safety lock that will not fly off if the pressure rises too high. This type of cooker seldom clogs and is easy to clean.

A cast-iron dutch oven is ideal for making tempura. I have one which I use exclusively for this purpose. If the pot is well-seasoned you can leave the oil in it, as long as you keep it tightly covered and stored in a dark place. The oil can also be stored in a tightly-covered glass jar. To clean your oil (and also for removing tempura), I suggest purchasing an oil skimmer, which is simply a wire mesh spoon. A Japanese skimmer, made of a bamboo handle with a wire basket attached, can also be used. For draining tempura, you can purchase wire drain racks which fit directly on the side of the pot.

I also suggest using a flame deflector for cooking rice and other foods such as soups, beans, or sauces. They distribute the flame evenly and prevent the food from burning and sticking. Simply place them under your pots when cooking.

Wooden utensils will not scratch your pots and pans nor leave a metallic taste in your food. Use them for sautéing and stirring. You should have at least two wooden spoons, a wooden rice paddle for removing rice from the pressure-cooker, and several pairs of cooking chopsticks.

A Japanese *suribachi*, or grinding bowl, is very handy in puréeing foods, making salad dressings, *gomasio*, seaweed condiments, and other items. A *suri-*

bachi is a ceramic bowl with grooves set into its surface and is used with a wooden pestle. Simply move the pestle in a spirallic motion when grinding.

A Foley hand food mill is useful for easy puréeing, when you are making pumpkin pies, squash soups, and other items. Electric blenders should be avoided whenever possible. They are very noisy and upset the quiet, peaceful atmosphere of your kitchen and the vibration of your food. For a large party or to save time, you may occasionally use one, but do not make them part of your day-to-day cooking.

A natural-bristle vegetable brush is important for cleaning root vegetables. This is especially true for organic vegetables, since they are often caked with heavy soil. Brush the vegetables firmly under running water to wash away the soil, but gently enough so as not to remove the skin. Unlike most supermarket vegetables that have been highly fertilized or waxed, organic vegetables need not be peeled. The skin is a valuable part of the vegetable and in macrobiotic cooking we try to use the whole food as much as possible.

Another important item in macrobiotic cooking is a good vegetable knife. A good, sharp knife enables you to cut your vegetables evenly, attractively, and quickly. There are many styles of cutting knives, and each has its advantages. A stainless steel knife, for instance, will not rust, but it chips easily and does not hold a sharp enough edge. There are two types of carbon steel knives, a low and a high grade. The low grade knife is useful, but unless it is properly dried and stored, it is liable to rust and chip. The higher grade knife will not rust. Carbon steel blades sharpen easily, hold an edge longer, and do not chip as easily as the stainless steel variety. I have found the high grade carbon steel knife, called the *Ai* knife, to be very efficient for cutting squash and other vegetables. It is slightly lighter than most carbon steel knives and is comfortable to use. It sharpens on one side, rather than both sides, thus insuring an even cut.

A sharpening stone is easy to use, and used regularly, will help maintain your knives' cutting edges. Oil your stone with sesame oil. To sharpen a knife, hold the handle firmly in your hand. Turn the knife on its side. Place the knife on the sharpening stone. Place your thumb, index and middle fingers on the side of the knife blade. Press down with your fingers firmly. Then push the blade of the knife away from you, until the entire length of the blade has run across the stone. Repeat two or three times. Then turn the knife blade over on its other side and repeat as above. To remove any burrs very lightly run the blade the length of the stone once.

Vegetables should be cut on a wooden board or chopping block. Wipe the board with a wet sponge before each use so that the water soaks into the wood. This will prevent the board from absorbing the juices from each vegetable. Also, occasionally oil your board with sesame oil to avoid warping or drying out. Wooden bowls should also be oiled with sesame oil occasionally to keep them from drying out and cracking. It is not advisable to use soap on wooden boards, bowls, or wooden utensils, as it is difficult to remove the taste of the soap from the wood. Fish leaves a very strong odor which is difficult to remove from wood unless you use soap. I suggest that you set aside a special board just for cutting fish.

A large strainer or colander is useful for washing grains, beans, seaweeds, seeds, and for draining noodles. Also, a small, fine mesh strainer is good for washing smaller items like millet or sesame seeds.

Baking dishes made of earthenware are very useful. They take longer to heat than glass, but hold heat well and require less water in baking. They are also easy to clean.

There is little need for soaps in a macrobiotic kitchen, except for very oily dishes, or in case you have burned a pot or have cooked fish. Vegetable oils seldom burn, unless you have the flame very high, and they wash off easily. If you do need soap, purchase a good quality, organic, biodegradable brand. Be sure to rinse your pots thoroughly in this case, as biodegradable soaps are a little harder to remove than regular soaps.

Gas stoves are the most practical cooking ranges in terms of being able to control the flame. They also create a more harmonious vibration in your food than do electric stoves. Electric ranges, besides responding less quickly to changes in heat, create a more chaotic vibration in your foods. Wood stoves are excellent, although it takes practice and patience to be able to regulate the temperature while cooking.

You may want to purchase several large glass jars for storing your grains, seeds, beans, nuts or dried foods. They are inexpensive and can be found in many natural food stores. Wood or ceramic containers are the best, as they allow air to circulate through the food. They may be difficult to find, however, and expensive.

The following items are also very useful in the kitchen:
   —A flat grater.
   —A bamboo strainer for straining *bancha* tea and other beverages.
   —A *tamari* dispenser, for pouring *tamari*.
   —Several bamboo *sushi* mats. These are made from thin strips of bamboo
      tied together with string, and are very good to use in covering food, as
      they allow heat to escape and air to enter so that it does not spoil quickly
      if unrefrigerated.

Of course, you may want to buy these items gradually as the need arises, since outfitting a kitchen can be expensive. But remember that the kitchen is the center of the home, the place where the family's health and happiness are established. Any investment in good quality cookware will pay for itself many times over.

I highly recommend that you never cook meat or animal foods other than fish in your pots and pans. These foods will destroy the pans' seasoning and upset their vibrational quality. Your other cooking utensils should be used only in preparing the best quality foods, in order to convey the highest quality energy possible to those who eat from your kitchen.

Preparation For Cooking

Enter your kitchen with a feeling of love for your family, your friends, and for society. Be humble. Think of the health and happiness you wish to bestow on those who will eat your meal. Most of all, keep your mind on your cooking. Become part of your kitchen in helping the food to cook itself.

When preparing food, forget about any problems or events that may have upset you that day. Cultivate a peaceful clear mind as you begin preparing the food.

Before you start to cook, wash your hands and, if you have long hair, tie it back so it does not get in your way or in the food. Put on a clean apron so as not to soil your clothing.

Avoid wearing perfume or cosmetics when cooking as the scent may interfere with your ability to perceive subtle differences in the odors of your foods, thus increasing the chance of burning your dishes.

Always begin cooking in a clean and orderly kitchen. Make sure that all of your dishes have been washed and put away in convenient places. As soon as you have finished with a pan or utensil, wash it so that you have space on your counter. You may also need to use a particular utensil again during your cooking and having to stop and wash it may mean the difference between a burned vegetable and a delicious one.

Listening to music while cooking will distract your concentration and upset your peaceful attitude. Also, you will be unable to hear your food cooking or the gauge on your pressure-cooker jiggling.

The food you prepare will absorb your mental energy. If you enter the kitchen with a clear, peaceful, and loving mind, your meal will vibrate with this energy. Dishes cooked in a chaotic or angry state will absorb those qualities and the people who eat them will become chaotic and angry.

Remember also that your physical, mental, and spiritual condition changes daily and that your cooking will reflect this change. Do not become discouraged if something doesn't turn out well. Simply search for the reasons why it happened and try again. Your skill will improve with practice, and as your condition improves.

The sooner you develop your common sense and intuition in cooking, the better and more efficient your cooking will be. Learn to rely on a cookbook as little as possible. Once you know proportions, begin experimenting with different combinations of foods. Be creative and artistic. Intuition means that instead of using a measuring cup or spoon, you use the amount that looks or tastes right. Trust your senses instead of utensils. Your cooking will take on a personal style based on your family's particular needs, as you decrease your reliance on recipes.

Use your cooking time efficiently. While you are washing rice, for instance, your seaweed could be soaking, and while waiting for the pressure-cooker to come down to pressure, wash dirty dishes or remove food from other pans, or put a garnish on completed dishes of food. Wasting time is a beginner's trait, and instills a feeling of disorderliness in your kitchen.

I have found simple cooking to be the best. This means not doing things like mixing a lot of vegetables together in one dish or using many different ingredients to create a casserole that tastes like something you used to like before you became macrobiotic. This type of cooking often creates unfavorable results. Each vegetable or grain has its own distinct flavor which you should try to enhance. When combining vegetables, use only a few, or if you use many, make sure they balance or complement each other. Cluttered dishes are not appetizing, and in general, do not foster health. Spices will weaken your health and ability to cook, and their use should be kept to a minimum. Use only enough seasoning to bring out the natural flavor of your grains, vegetables, and other foods. Heavy seasoning overcomes the natural, wholesome taste of foods.

A good macrobiotic cook is never completely satisfied with her ability. Even though your cooking improves year after year, you should always feel that there is more to learn and that your ability can always be improved. Strive to refine your style by eating other people's cooking, taking classes and reading and studying books on macrobiotic cooking. Even if you don't totally agree with another cook's style, you will learn things that will help in your cooking.

Washing Grains, Beans, Seeds, Vegetables and Seaweed

Always wash your food well. Grains that are naturally processed often contain grit which must be removed. Can you imagine how unpleasant it is to bite into a stone or find small worms or bugs floating in your soup? Washing removes dust and impurities and helps to make your food tasty.

Before washing grains, place a handful at a time on a plate. Pick out any stones or large pieces of soil. Then put the grain in a pot or bowl and cover with water. Wash the grain by gently stirring with your hand in a counter-clockwise direction, and then drain off the water. Repeat this three or more times until the water becomes almost clear. It is important to wash your food quickly so that its natural sweetness is not lost in the rinsing process. Afterwards, place the grain in a colander or strainer and rinse quickly to remove any smaller particles of dust which may remain. The grains are then ready to be placed in a pressure-cooker or pot, to which the appropriate amount of water and salt is then added.

When washing seeds, such as sesame seeds, first remove the small stones by hand, then place in a fine mesh strainer and rinse well to remove dust.

When washing beans, first pick out any stones or large chunks of soil and then place the beans in a pot or bowl. Add water, and wash in the same way as grains. Repeat twice. Then, place them in a colander or strainer and rinse again. Your beans are now ready to cook.

Root vegetables, like carrots, burdock, *daikon* and turnips, among others, require the use of a vegetable brush to remove soil. Scrub firmly but gently, being careful not to remove the skin. Onions are peeled by first cutting off the bottom root and then the top stem. Wash in cold running water after peeling. Onions ready for cooking should be shiny and should squeak when you run your fingers across them.

All grains, vegetables, beans, seeds, and seaweeds should be washed in cold water.

Leafy green vegetables, such as broccoli, bok choy, chard, kale, and others, should be washed thoroughly under cold water. Kale has very fine, jagged leaves, and dirt and dried leaves easily adhere to them. Organic broccoli often contains worms that are the same color as the stem, and insects that look like tiny spiders. They are the same color as the broccoli flower, and can be mistaken for these little flowerettes. Watercress should be washed by putting it in a pot or bowl and covering with water. Rinee, pour off the water, and repeat this process three times. Then, run each piece of watercress under cold water. Watercress often has little eels or snails in it which proper washing will remove.

Seaweeds such as *hijiki* and *arame* should be lightly rinsed and then soaked before using. Rinsing seaweeds too long, however, will wash away much of their flavor and minerals. Seaweeds only need to be soaked for 3–5 minutes, and this soaking water can be used when preparing seaweeds or soups with seaweed in them. *Kombu* does not need to be washed. However, if you want to remove some of the salt, lightly brush it with a wet sponge. *Wakame* can be quickly rinsed and then soaked in the same way as *arame* or *hijiki*. *Nori* does not need to be washed at all. It should be roasted by holding the glossy side about 10 inches above the flame on your stove until it is evenly toasted. This takes only about 10–12 seconds.

Squash should be scrubbed with a vegetable brush. For varieties such as buttercup, butternut, hubbard, and Hokkaido pumpkin, first scrub with a vegetable brush, then cut the squash and remove the seeds with a spoon. If you wish to save the seeds, wash the pulp from them and place them on a plate or bamboo mat to dry for a couple of days. The seeds, once dry, can be sprinkled with a little *tamari* and roasted in the oven to be eaten as a snack. You can also save the seeds after drying and store in a tightly sealed jar for planting in the spring, or set them out for the birds.

Grains, beans, and seeds may be stored for short periods in glass jars. When storing grains in glass containers it is advisable to stir the grain occasionally. This circulates air through the grain and allows it to breathe. Also, stirring helps to reduce the possibility of moths or bugs incubating in the jars. Keep your grains stored in a cool, dry room.

Wooden or ceramic containers are the best to store dry foods in as they allow the food to receive fresh air. Food may be stored for long periods in these types of containers.

When storing grains, beans, and seeds, you may insert several bay leaves into the jars or barrels. This reduces the possibility of moths and bugs appearing in the food.

Seaweeds should be kept in glass jars or plastic bags. Seaweeds are dry and salty and will absorb moisture from the air if stored in paper bags.

Seasonings such as *tamari, miso*, and sea salt should be stored in tightly sealed glass jars and kept in a cool, shaded or dark cupboard. Occasionally, *miso* will develop a mold on top. If this happens, simply mix it in with the rest of the *miso*. It is not harmful, since *miso* is a live, fermented food, created by bacterial action. If *miso* is stored in a tightly sealed glass jar and is kept in a warm place such as the kitchen for several weeks, I have found that it turns sour. It should be stored in a cool but not freezing room.

Uncovered sea salt will form into large cakes, because it has no sugar or chemicals to keep it from absorbing moisture from the air. Oil can be stored for several months in clear or dark-colored jars that are tightly sealed.

During the summer months, when fresh vegetables are plentiful, try to buy only enough for one week, or if possible, buy your vegetables daily. They will keep best in the refrigerator or in a dark, cool room.

During the winter, many vegetables can be easily stored. If you have a cool, dry room in your basement you can build storage bins and shelves. Squash can be stored for a good part of the winter on shelves. Make sure that they do not touch each other, as this will cause spoilage. Also, the stems should be left on the squash to prolong shelf life.

Root vegetables, such as carrots, burdock, *daikon*, turnips, and onions can be stored in bins filled with damp sand, leaves, or sawdust. When storing vegetables in sand, place them right side up and cover the tops. When storing in dry leaves or sawdust, the vegetables can be layered. When storing onions for the winter it is best to sort the onions and group them together according to size and use the smaller ones up first as they tend to dry faster. Whenever you notice vegetables beginning to go soft or decay, immediately remove them so that they do not spoil the other vegetables. Water should occasionally be sprinkled on the sand or vegetables to prevent drying out. All vegetables and fruits should be stored in a cool, dry place.

If you wish to store cabbage, make sure you buy those with the root still attached. Tie a piece of string or twine around the root and then hang each cabbage upside down with the other end of the string tied to a nail driven into a beam in your cellar.

Apples will keep very well if they are stored in a cool place. Varieties such as MacIntosh, Cortland, Red Delicious, etc. keep for two to four months. Rome, Baldwin, Northern Spy, etc. will keep two or three months longer. They should be kept in crates and placed in a cool, dry room.

Root vegetables, such as *daikon*, burdock, or carrots can also be dried in a shaded place. For variety you may also want to shred *daikon* and carrots and leave them out to dry. Once they are dry, store them in tightly sealed containers. Vegetables become very sweet when dried. Fruits can be sliced and dried in the same manner.

Pickling is another natural way of storing vegetables Recipes for making various pickles are given in a later chapter.

Greens are an important part of our daily diet and, if possible, should be purchased regularly throughout the year, at a natural foods store or supermarket.

Oil

The best quality oils for use in cooking and baking are sesame and corn oil. There are two types of sesame oil: light and dark. Dark sesame oil is made from roasted sesame seeds and has a rich, delicious flavor. The light oil is made from raw seeds. I use the dark variety more during the winter than the summer, as it has a slightly heavier taste than the light oil. Light sesame oil can be used year-round. Corn oil, I have found, is the best for making pastries and cookies, while light sesame oil is better in making bread.

Unlike the commercial brands of oil found in supermarkets, the sesame and corn oil sold in natural food stores are made by a process called "cold-pressing." This means that the seeds have been mechanically pressed at a temperature below the boiling point, thus keeping all the nutrients intact. These oils contain no chemical solvents and are not bleached.

Most commercial vegetable oils are steamed at a temperature of more than twice the boiling point of water, which destroys vitamin E, as well as other vitamins. They are then treated with petroleum-based chemical solvents, which make it possible to squeeze more oil from each seed or grain. The oil is later bleached and deodorized. Commerically produced oils are a major factor in the cause of various modern illnesses.

Vitamin E prevents oils from turning rancid. This is why commercial oils spoil easily, and why cold-pressed oils do not.

Also, cold-pressed oils taste more like the seed or grain from which they are produced, whereas commercial oils have very little taste resemblance to the original seed or grain.

Cold-pressed oils cost more than commercial brands, but any added expense is more than compensated for with better health. Be careful however, about the amount of oil that you eat, even if it is of good quality. The body needs a certain amount to help build new cells and tissues and to keep warm, but remember that grains and beans, as well as many other foods, contain oil, and that it is easy to take too much if you are not careful.

Skin and intestinal problems can result from consuming oil in excess of your body's needs. Many people suffer from liver, gall bladder, and stomach disorders because of too much oil in their diet. Individual needs for oil vary and, as a cook, you should take this into consideration.

Cutting Vegetables

In macrobiotic cooking, the cutting of vegetables in the appropriate size, shape, and thickness is very important, both in terms of balancing the yin and yang factors, and in making your meals appealing and delicious. Treat vegetables gently and with appreciation, and not as if you were handling a piece of wood. Vegetables should be sliced in a smooth, natural stroke rather than chopped. A sharp knife is essential for this function.

The proper cutting technique is to hold the vegetable with your fingers curled slightly at the first knuckle, placing the blade against your knuckles, thus minimizing the possibility of cutting your fingers and nails. Then, place the front part of the blade on the vegetable and slide it firmly but gently forward through the vegetable, using the entire length of the blade. Do not saw or push down through the vegetable. Remember, your vegetables are alive and should be treated with respect. If they are handled in a disruptive or chaotic fashion, the vegetables will absorb and convey this energy to those who eat them. Food is our primary means of establishing and maintaining health and happiness. When preparing and eating meals we should treat our food with the respect it deserves.

Diagonal (*Hasugiri*):   Hold knife at angle and cut on a diagonal. By changing the angle of the blade you can change the length of the sliced vegetable.

Triangular (*Rangiri*):   Reverse directions of diagonal slice thus creating triangular wedges.

Half Moons (*Hangetsu*):   Cut lengthwise through center into halves. Then cut as for thin rounds.

Diced (*Sainome*): Cut vegetable into 1/4 to 1/2 inch cubes.

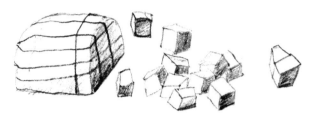

Matchsticks (*Sengiri*): Cut on diagonal. Cut each diagonal into matchstick-sized pieces.

Chrysanthemums (*Kikukagiri*): Cut vegetable into 1 to 1-1/2 inch thick rounds. Cut several slices across rounds. Leave attached at base. Turn vegetable around and cut across in opposite direction, at same width and depth. Soak cut rounds in cold water before cooking to open the flowers.

Rectangles (*Tanzaku*): Cut into 1 to 2 inch rounds, then cut each round into four or five 1/4 to 1/3 inch pieces. Then each section into thin rectangles.

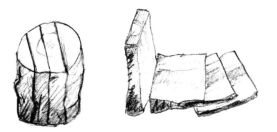

Quarters: Cut lengthwise into halves. Then cut each half lengthwise again. Then slice as for rounds.

Cutting Leaves: Stack two or three leaves on top of each other. Cut through center along spine of leaf. Cut each halved leaf on a diagonal into 1/8 to 1/4 inch strips.

Dicing Onions (*Mijingiri*): Cut onion in half. Cut thin parallel slices across onion leaving attached at root base. Then slice in opposite direction to root base. Then dice root base into small pieces.

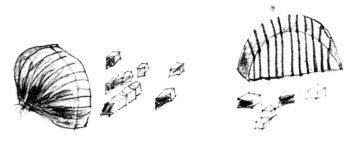

Onion Half Moons: Cut in half. Then cut each half into thin slices.

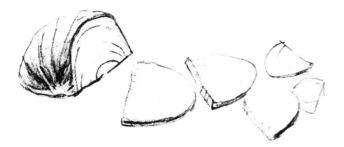

Flower Shapes (*Hanagata*): Cut four or five lengthwise wedges at equal distances around the vegetable. Then slice into thin rounds.

Shaving (*Sasagaki*): Place knife at bottom of root vegetable and shave as you would a pencil or piece of wood. Rotate vegetable slightly as you shave. Shave thick or thin by changing the angle of the knife.

Rounds (*Koguchigiri*): Cut on diagonal, into thin rounds or thick (*wagiri*) rounds.

Rolling Method for Irregular Wedges (*Mawashigiri*):   Cut on a diagonal, rotating vegetable toward you. Rotate 1/4 turn (90 degrees), slice, rotate 1/4 turn, slice again. Repeat, creating a shape that is triangular with a rounded base.

We usually cut vegetables diagonally so that each piece will contain both yin and yang parts. When combining vegetables cut each variety into pieces of a general size and thickness, so that they will all be cooked at the same time. Each piece should be bite-sized, so that they are not awkward to eat. With practice, your knife technique will improve, thus enhancing the appearance of your dishes and substantially reducing the time involved in preparation.

Salt

The proper use of salt in cooking is essential in creating health and happiness.

There is much controversy today over the use of salt. Some people do not use it at all because of high blood pressure or other problems, while others consume, perhaps unknowingly, large quantities contained in various animal products, besides adding it in cooking or at the table. Obviously, vegetarians or semi-vegetarians, whose diet is low in the hidden salts contained in animal food, can take more salt than persons who have a history of animal food consumption. For example, until recently, the Japanese based their diet on grains, vegetables, beans, seaweeds, and some fish and did not eat much meat or dairy food. Naturally, they are generally able to tolerate larger amounts of salt than many Americans.

Our use of salt should vary, depending on climate, environment, mental or physical activities, sex, and other factors. Also, each person's basic constitution is different, so each of us differs in our tolerance level for salt. A robust, hardy individual may need less salt, for example, than a person with a weaker constitution. Also, if the climate in which you live is more humid and wet, or cold, you may be able to take more than a person living in a dry or hot climate. But, despite these variables, our bodies need a certain minimum amount of salt in order to keep the intestines and muscles firm, to help to digest food, and to keep the body warm.

The salt sold in the supermarket has most of its trace minerals removed. It is, in fact, 99.9 % sodium chloride. It is also iodized because science has found that iodine apparently helps in the formation of thyroid hormones. Iodized salt contains, of all things, sugar, to make it pour easily and to keep the iodine from breaking down. Sodium bicarbonate is also added to iodized salt as a bleaching agent to keep the salt white.

The salt used in macrobiotic cooking is taken from sea water and sun-dried or baked in kilns. It has approximately 12% trace minerals and 88% sodium chloride. Sea salt does not pour well because it has no sugar in it, nor are iodine or sodium bicarbonate added. Iodine can easily be obtained by eating seaweeds which can be deliciously prepared.

When using salt in cooking, add only enough to bring out the sweetness and natural flavor of foods. Your meals should never taste salty. It takes practice to master the use of salt and experience to become sensitive to your own needs. If you take too much you will feel irritable, angry, hyperactive, and thirsty. You may also retain liquid, thus feeling bloated, and you may have a tendency to over-eat, which can lead to laziness and inactivity.

Children need much less salt than adults, as they are already very yang —small, compact, and active. If you give them too much salt, they will become irritable, angry, cruel, overactive, and may cry a lot. Excess salt can also cause children to grit their teeth or sleep with their eyes open. Babies need no salt until about the age of six months, and even then only a couple of grains added to their rice or vegetables. As they grow older, gradually increase the amount, but the quantity should be much less than for adults.

Another sign of too much salt is loss of weight, which produces a gaunt appearance, as well as lower back pains from contracted kidneys and muscle tissues.

A lack of salt can produce such symptoms as sluggishness, spaciness, lack of mental clarity, diarrhea, sleepiness, yawning, and poor circulation. Salt deficiency in children is manifested in inactivity, laziness, constant whining and complaining as well as any of the already-mentioned signs.

These are only a few of the symptoms resulting from too little or too much salt. You may experience others, such as craving yin foods like fruits, desserts, or other sweets if you eat too much salt. Also, if a person consumes too much salt he often begins to crave protein because the body has to maintain a 1-to-7 ratio of minerals to protein.

The only foods which should have a salty taste are the condiments which are added to your food after it has been cooked. These should be used according to personal taste. In general, condiments should be used moderately. Children should have special condiments such as *gomasio* with a ratio of at least 20 parts seeds to 1 part salt, roasted seaweed powder, and, if they are attracted to putting *tamari* on their food, a special bottle filled with a half-*tamari*-half-water combination. Try putting these special condiments in a container with their name written or taped on it. They will love seeing their name on their own special jar of *tamari* or *gomasio*! You can continue to do this until they are old enough to understand that they need less salt than adults.

Cooking during the winter needs to be slightly more salty than in the hot summer months, as the body needs more salt to generate warmth. We also need a little bit more oil in the winter for the same reason.

Some of the recipes in this book recommend using 1/4 to 1/2 teaspoon salt. Please keep in mind that these are only general suggestions. In the summer, or for a more yang person, use less, while for a more yin person or during the winter, use slightly more.

Be flexible and experiment to discover the amount of salt that you or your family feel comfortable with. If you experience any of the above symptoms of too much or too little salt, adjust your intake accordingly. Remember also that your family's condition is continually changing in response to fluctuating environmental, social and personal circumstances. A recipe that may be just right today may be inappropriate a week from now. Flexibility in your thinking and in your cooking is essential.

Grains including Seitan and Noodles

Brown Rice

Be selective when buying brown rice. A large percentage of green grains in the rice indicates that it is not yet mature, while rice that is broken or chipped has not been properly milled. Rice in this condition begins to oxidize from exposure to the air, resulting in the disruption of its natural balance of carbohydrates, minerals, and vitamins. It is already starting to lose its *ki* or life energy. Rice that has been grown and milled properly is vibrant with a life force that will remain intact for thousands of years, and even if then planted, will sprout and grow.

In terms of yin and yang, rice is the most balanced of all the grains. This is reflected in its natural balance of minerals, protein, and carbohydrates. This is one reason why brown rice is the most suitable grain for daily consumption. Also, it is the most biologically developed grain. Since mankind is the most biologically developed species in the animal kingdom we should eat our counterpart in the vegetable world.

Cereal grains should comprise 50% to 60% of your daily food, and brown rice should be your main or primary grain. It should be eaten every day and the other grains should be used as supplemental side dishes. If you eat brown rice daily, your condition will improve rapidly, and you will automatically become happy, healthy, and satisfied in whatever you are doing.

I highly recommend that you avoid cracked grains as much as possible. They are not whole foods and, if eaten regularly, tend to create mucus in the body and can cause cloudy thinking.

Pressure-cooking is the best way to prepare brown rice. Your rice will cook quickly and thoroughly, and will taste sweet when made this way. Pressure-cooked rice will accelerate your physical, mental and spiritual development to an extent no other cooking method can.

We should continually reflect on the quality of our cooking technique. If our family does not eat much rice, then something is wrong with our preparation. Our condition changes daily and thus the way in which we cook rice will also change. Always try to improve your rice. If, for example, it is burnt on the bottom, the flame may be too high, so lower it the next time you cook. The flame may not be high enough if the rice is too wet. Dry rice indicates that you probably did not use enough water, and if your rice is too mushy, you have probably used too much. Your rice should be well cooked and each grain should be separate. It should taste sweet and become sweeter the more you chew it. Needless to say, all of your food should be thoroughly chewed, to the point where it becomes liquified, before you swallow. Grains are digested primarily in the mouth through their interaction with saliva. If they are not well chewed they can not be properly digested.

Never fill the pot more than half with grain when pressure-cooking rice and other grains. This will bring the cooker to about 70% of its capacity after water has been added. If you put too much grain in the pressure-cooker, it will not cook as well.

Pressure-Cooked Brown Rice

> **1 cup brown rice**
> **1-1/4 to 1-1/2 cups water per cup of rice**
> **pinch of sea salt per cup of rice**

Wash rice as explained previously. Place rice in pressure-cooker. Add water and salt. Place cover on pressure-cooker and turn the flame to high. When the gauge begins to hiss or jiggle remove pot from flame, put a flame deflector on top of the burner and then place pressure-cooker on top of a flame deflector. Reduce flame to medium-low and cook for 45–50 minutes. When rice is done, remove from burner and allow pressure to come down naturally.

This will take approximately 15–20 minutes, depending upon how many cups of rice you have cooked. Before removing the top from the pressure-cooker, lift the gauge to make sure that the pressure has come completely down. Remove cover. Remove rice from pot with a bamboo rice paddle, one spoonful at a time, and smooth each spoonful into a wooden bowl, so that the bottom (most yang) and the top (most yin) part of the rice are evenly distributed.

Another way to prepare rice is, instead of turning the flame high, to bring the pressure up, gradually increase the flame from low to high, taking 15 minutes. This gives the rice a very delicious flavor and peaceful feeling.

Boiled Brown Rice

> 1 cup rice
> 2 cups water
> pinch of sea salt

Wash rice and place in heavy pot. Add water and salt. Cover with a heavy lid. Bring to boil, lower flame to medium-low and simmer for one hour or until all water has been absorbed. Remove and serve.

Soft Brown Rice (Rice *Kayu*)

> 1 cup rice
> 5 cups water
> pinch of sea salt

Wash rice. Cook as for pressure-cooked or boiled rice, but in this case not all of the water will be absorbed. Contents should be creamy and contain whole grains of rice. This makes a tasty breakfast cereal and is recommended for people who have digestive problems or any other type of sickness.

For variety, you can add vegetables such as Chinese cabbage or *daikon*, or even an *umeboshi* plum while cooking.

Fried Rice

> 4 cups cooked rice
> 1 Tbsp. sesame oil
> 1 medium onion sliced diagonally or diced
> 1–2 Tbsp. tamari soy sauce

Brush skillet lightly with oil. Heat and add onion. Place rice on top of onion. (If rice is dry add a few drops of water to moisten.) Place cover on skillet and cook on low flame for 10–15 minutes. Add *tamari* and cook 5–10 minutes longer. Make sure to keep the flame low or the onions will burn. There is no need to stir, so do not mix until just before serving. Mix and serve hot.

As a variation, use scallions, parsley, or a combination of vegetables such as onions and carrots, *daikon* and *daikon* leaves, onions and beans, Chinese cabbage and mushrooms, or onions and celery.

Pressure-Cooked Rice with Beans

1 cup rice
10 % beans*(see below)
1-1/4 to 1-1/2 cups water
pinch of sea salt

Wash grain and beans. Cook beans as mentioned below. Add beans and cooking water to rice after they have cooled. The cooking water from the beans should be counted as part of the 1-1/4 to 1-1/2 cups of water in the recipe. Pressure-cook 45–50 minutes, and remove as with plain rice.

*Azuki, kidney, or pinto beans should first be cooked 1/2 hour, allowed to cool and then added with their cooking water to rice.

Chickpeas should be soaked overnight, then cooked for 1/2 hours, allowed to cool, then added to rice with cooking water.

Black beans (Japanese soybeans) should be soaked in salt water several hours and then boiled 1/2 hour. Skim the gray foam from the beans as it rises to the surface. Cool and add beans and cooking water to rice.

Brown Rice with Chestnuts

1 cup rice
10 % dried chestnuts
1-1/4 to 1-1/2 cups water
pinch of sea salt

Wash rice. It is easy to remove the dark skin of the chestnuts if they are first soaked or roasted in a dry skillet on a low flame for several minutes or so. Add to rice and cook as with plain pressure-cooked rice.

Rice may be cooked with vegetables, vegetable water, soaking water from *kombu*, *wakame*, or *shiitake* mushrooms, or with *bancha* tea. When using *bancha* tea instead of plain water add a couple of drops of *tamari* soy sauce in in addition to the correct proportion of sea salt. There are thousands of variations that you can create when cooking rice. Please use your imagination to prepare appetizing and delicious rice throughout the year.

Sushi

Sushi is a traditional Japanese dish. It makes an attractive party treat, and is nice for picnics, while traveling, or for special meals.

nori
cooked brown rice
carrot cut into strips
scallion leaves
umeboshi or umeboshi paste

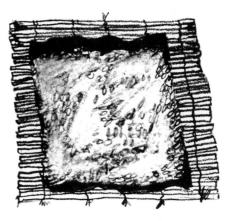

Step 1: Roast one side of a sheet of *nori* over a flame until it turns green, and place on a bamboo *sushi* mat. Wet your hands with water, and spread cooked brown rice evenly on the sheet of *nori*. Leave about 1/2 to 1 inch of the top edge of *nori* and about 1/8 to 1/4 inch of the bottom edge uncovered.

Step 2: Slice a carrot into lengthwise strips that are 8 to 10 inches long and about 1/4 inch thick and boil with a pinch of sea salt for 2 to 3 minutes. When the carrots are just slightly crisp, remove and allow to cool. Separate the green leaf portion of several scallions from the roots so that each strip is about 8 to 10 inches in length. Place carrot and scallion strips approximately 1/2 to 1 inch from the bottom of the sheet of *nori*. Then lightly spread 1/16 to 1/8 teaspoon puréed *umeboshi* along the entire length of the carrot and scallion strips.

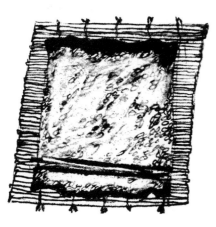

Step 3: Pressing the *sushi* mat firmly against the rice and *nori*, roll it into a log shape. The vegetables should be centered in the roll. If they are not, they were probably placed too far from the bottom edge of the *nori* and rice. Wet edge of the *nori* to seal the roll.

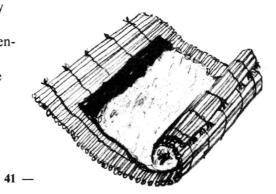

Step 4: Wet a very sharp knife and slice the roll into rounds approximately 1/2 to 1 inch thick. You may need to wet the knife each time you slice. The roll will not slice properly if you do not wet your knife after each cut. In this case the *nori* will often tear and the rice may stick to the knife.

Step 5: Arrange rounds on a platter with the cut side up, showing the rice and vegetables.

As a variation, you can put strips of fish, pickles, deep-fried *tofu*, or other root or green vegetables in the *sushi*. If you are going on a trip or picnic, or if it is a hot day, *umeboshi* plums or other pickles will help keep the rice from spoiling. Leftover *sushi* that has become slightly sour or dry can be deep-fried in hot sesame oil to make a delicious crunchy snack.

For a variation, you can also make *sushi* with *soba* noodles instead of rice.

Millet

Millet is one of the most widely used cereal grains. It still forms a major part of the diet of about one-third of the world's population, particularly in China, Japan, Korea, India, and Africa. Millet is especially good for problems relating to the stomach, spleen and pancreas. We use it quite often in our home as a supplement to rice.

Millet with Vegetables

    1 cup millet
    1 onion sliced diagonally
    1 carrot cut in matchsticks
    3 cups boiling water
    sesame oil
    pinch of sea salt per cup of millet

Wash millet in fine mesh strainer. Brush pot lightly with sesame oil. (If you wish to avoid oil eliminate sautéing, although you can still roast the millet in a dry skillet for a nutty flavor.) Sauté vegetables for 3 to 5 minutes on low flame. Add millet to vegetables and sauté for 3 to 5 minutes longer. Add boiling water and salt. Bring to a boil. Turn flame low, cover, and simmer for 30–35 minutes or until water is absorbed.

Soft Millet

Use the same method as above, but add 4 cups of boiling water instead of 3. This makes a very good breakfast cereal.

Oats

Oats are related to rice and barley and are high in vitamin B, protein, and minerals. A clear indication of the dietary practices in the United States is seen in the fact that 95% of the oats grown in this country are fed to animals, while humans consume only 5% of the total crop. This grain makes a delicious morning cereal, and can also be used in making desserts and pie crusts. When shopping in a natural food store, you will notice three types: whole oats, steel cut oats, which have been steamed and cut into pieces, and rolled oats, which have been steamed and rolled.

Whole Oats

> **1 cup whole oats**
> **5–6 cups water**
> **pinch of sea salt**

Wash oats and place in pot. Add water and salt. (Roasting the oats in a dry skillet until light gold produces a nutty flavor.) Cover and bring to a boil. Reduce flame and simmer on a very low flame for several hours or overnight. Place a flame deflector under pot to prevent burning. This dish makes an excellent breakfast cereal.

Rolled Oats

> **1 cup rolled oats**
> **2–3 cups water**
> **pinch of sea salt**

Roast oats over a low flame for several minutes until they release a nutty fragrance if you wish to change the flavor somewhat, or you can use them as they come from the store. Add water and salt and bring to a boil. Cover and reduce flame to low and simmer for 30 minutes.

You can add a sliced onion for variety.

Buckwheat or Kasha

Traditionally, buckwheat was used as a staple food in Russia and Central Europe. It is the most yang of the cereal grains and is very high in calcium, vitamin B, iron, and minerals. For example, my husband's grandmother, Mrs. Esuchenko, was raised on a farm in what is now Poland. She would often reminisce about *kasha* which was a regular part of her family's diet. In Japan, it is mainly used in making a type of noodle called *soba*. In cold weather, this grain can be used occasionally as a morning cereal or as a supplement to rice. It can also be used in making soup. Because it is such a yang grain, buckwheat should be used primarily in the winter and only in moderate quantities. *Soba* noodles are the exception and can be eaten year round.

You will notice that there are two types of buckwheat sold in most natural food stores—roasted and unroasted. The roasted variety need only to be re-roasted for about 3–5 minutes. To prepare the unroasted type, simply place in a dry skillet and roast for approximately 10 minutes or until dark brown, before cooking.

Kasha

> 1 cup buckwheat
> 2 cups boiling water
> pinch of sea salt

Place buckwheat in a dry skillet and roast 4–5 minutes. Put the grain in pot and add boiling water and salt. Bring to a boil, reduce flame and cover. Simmer for 30 minutes or until the water has been absorbed.

For variety, sauté cabbage and carrots or onions and chopped parsley in a very small amount of sesame oil. Add buckwheat, salt, and boiling water. Cook as above.

For a morning cereal add 4–5 cups of boiling water and cook as above.

Stuffed Cabbage

> 1 cup buckwheat
> 1/2 cup diced onion
> 1/2 cup diced carrot
> 1/4 cup diced mushrooms
> 1/4 cup chopped celery

4 cabbage leaves
2 cups boiling water
pinch of sea salt

Remove four whole cabbage leaves from a head of cabbage and boil until tender but not soft. Set aside to cool.

Brush pot lightly with sesame oil. Heat pot, add onion, carrot, mushrooms, and celery. Sauté for 5–10 minutes. Add buckwheat and mix with vegetables. Add boiling water and salt and bring to a boil. Cover the pan and reduce flame to low. Simmer 20–30 minutes. Remove from flame and allow to cool. Cut cabbage leaves from the core as shown in drawing. Place a large spoonful of kasha and vegetables in hand and form into a croquette. Place croquette on cabbage leaf. Fold sides of cabbage leaf toward center and roll into a croquette shape. Fasten leaf with a toothpick. Place cabbage in pot and add enough water to half-cover the stuffed cabbage. Add a couple of teaspoons of *tamari* to the water and bring to a boil. Cover, reduce flame to low and simmer for 20–25 minutes. Serve plain or with a bechamel sauce.

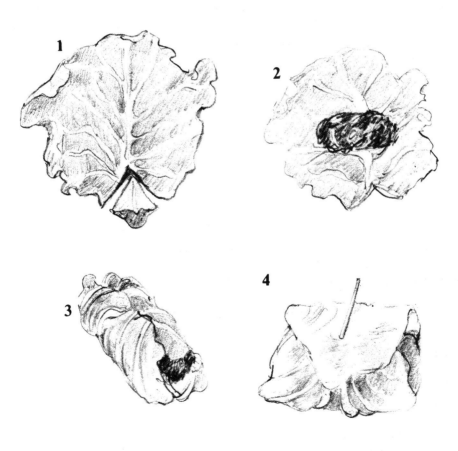

Sweet Rice

Sweet rice is more glutinous than regular brown rice. Traditionally it is used in Japan to make *sake*, an alcoholic beverage, and for making *mochi*, which is pounded into a sticky mass and formed into cakes. Sweet rice is high in protein and vitamin B. It is a delicious grain and may be eaten by itself or occasionally mixed with brown rice.

> **1 cup sweet rice**
> **1 cup water**
> **pinch of sea salt**

Wash rice. Add water and salt. Cook as for regular pressure-cooked brown rice.

Mochi

Cook same as above. After the pressure has come down, place rice in a wooden bowl. Pound the cooked rice with a heavy wooden pestle or *mochi* pounder (which can be purchased at a natural food store) until the grains are crushed and become very sticky. (Wet the *mochi* pounder occasionally during use to prevent rice from sticking to it.) Wet your hands and form a tablespoon of rice into a small ball or round cake. Or you can spread the *mochi* on a baking sheet which has been oiled and dusted with rice flour, and allow it to dry. To serve, cut into pieces and deep-fry, bake, or pan-fry in a dry skillet over a low flame. Pieces of *mochi* can also be added to hot *tamari* broth or *miso* soup a few minutes before serving the soup.

Ohagi

Cook, pound, and form sweet rice into cakes as mentioned above. These cakes can then be rolled in roasted sesame seeds, roasted and ground walnuts, or coated with *azuki* beans or chestnut purée to make delicious party snacks.

Seitan

Seitan is made from the gluten of hard spring or hard winter wheat flour and is very high in protein, calcium and niacin. It is a traditional food eaten in many countries throughout the world. *Seitan* can be used in soups, stews, salads, cooked with vegetables, in *sukiyaki*, sandwiches, or combined with bread crumbs, onions, celery and mushrooms to stuff a squash. There are many different ways of preparing this food.

I have found that the spring wheat flour produces a much softer texture of *seitan* than the winter wheat variety. In addition, it is easier to wash the bran from spring wheat flour. Both types produce the same amount of *seitan*.

There is a surprisingly quick method of making *seitan* that results in the same quality product that you would obtain by following the long method described in most macrobiotic cookbooks.

Seitan

3-1/2 lbs. whole wheat flour
8–9 cups water

Place flour in a large pot. Add enough warm water (8–9 cups) to make it the consistency of oatmeal or oatmeal cookie batter. Knead for 3–5 minutes or until the flour is thoroughly mixed with water. Cover with warm water and let sit for 5–10 minutes. (This is the minimum soaking time. The dough can stay in the water longer.) Knead again in the soaking water for about 1 minute. The water will turn cloudy or milky. Pour off the cloudy water into a jar. Save the soaking and the majority of the rinsing water. Place sticky gluten into a large strainer and put the strainer into a large pot or bowl. Pour cold water over the gluten and knead in the strainer. Repeat until the bran and starch are washed out. Alternate between warm and cold water when you are rinsing and kneading the gluten. This alternating water temperature makes washing out the bran easier. The first and last rinse should always be with cold water to contract the gluten into a large ball. Save the rinse liquid and use as a thickening agent for stews or gravies, or, if allowed to sour for 3–4 days, you can use it as a starter to make bread.

After you have rinsed and kneaded the bran and starch out of the gluten, wash it again in a bowl for 2–3 minutes with cold water to remove any remaining bran. The gluten should form a sticky ball. Separate the gluten into 5–6 pieces and form balls. Drop balls into 6 cups of boiling water, and boil for 5 minutes or until the balls float to the top. Remove and cut into cubes for soup or into strips if you plan to sauté it with vegetables. If you intend to make stuffed cabbage rolls or sandwiches with the *seitan*, leave the cooked pieces whole. Place one 3-inch strip of *kombu* in the boiling water and add 1/4 to 1/3 cup of *tamari*. Place cubed, sliced or whole pieces of gluten into the *tamari* water. Bring to a boil. Reduce flame to low, cover pot, and simmer for 35 to 45 minutes.

Seitan Stew

1 medium onion sliced
2 carrots (cut by rolling method)
1 stalk burdock sliced
1 cup brussels sprouts cut in half
1/4 cup sliced celery

All the seitan and the water from cooking the seitan in the above recipe and 1–2 cups seitan starch water (from rinsing seitan).

Cook *seitan* as above. When *seitan* has cooked for 35–45 minutes, add onions, carrots, burdock, brussels sprouts and celery. Add enough cold water, if needed, to cover the vegetables. Bring to a boil. Reduce flame to low and simmer until vegetables are done. Add starch water to make the consistency of a stew. Bring to a boil. Reduce flame to low. Add *tamari* to taste and simmer for 15–20 minutes. Add more starch water if the stew is too thin, or, if it is too thick, add more cold water.

Seitan-Barley Soup

  1/2 cup barley
  1 medium onion sliced
  2 carrots cut in irregular or rolling-method shape
  1/2 cup sliced mushrooms
  1/4 cup sliced celery

Wash barley, then boil it in 4 cups water. Reduce flame and simmer for 20–30 minutes. Add onions, carrots, mushrooms, and celery. Cook 15–20 minutes. Add *seitan* and *seitan tamari* water from above recipe. Bring to a boil. Reduce flame to low and simmer for 15–20 minutes. Add *tamari* to taste and simmer for 5–10 minutes.

Sautéed Vegetables and Seitan

Cook *seitan* in *tamari*, water and *kombu* as above. Remove *seitan* from water and slice. Add *seitan* slices to kale and carrots and sauté for 2 to 3 minutes. Add 1/4 cup *seitan tamari* water and simmer until kale and carrots are tender.

Stuffed Cabbage with Seitan

When cooking *seitan* in *tamari* water, as described above, leave the gluten in large pieces, approximately 2 inches by 2 inches in size, and boil as described earlier. Boil several cabbage leaves until almost tender. Remove from water, wrap *seitan* inside the cabbage leaves and fasten shut with a toothpick. Place one 3-inch piece of *kombu* in bottom of a skillet. Place cabbage rolls on top. Add 1 cup of water and 1 tablespoon *tamari*. Cover and bring to a boil. Reduce flame and simmer for 20–30 minutes.

Seitan Croquettes

When the bran and starch have been rinsed from the gluten as explained above, instead of boiling, separate the gluten into 5 equal pieces and form into balls. Pull the gluten into flat pieces and wrap one 2-inch-long × 1/8-inch-wide piece of carrot and burdock inside each piece. Deep-fry in hot oil until gluten is golden brown. Remove and place on a paper towel to drain. Cover bottom of a pot with a piece of *kombu*. Place pieces of deep-fried gluten on top and cover with water. Add two tablespoons of *tamari*. Bring to a boil. Reduce flame, cover, and simmer for 30–45 minutes.

To make a sauce, add 4 cups starch water to 1/2 cup diced onions and stir gently. Add 1 tablespoon *tamari* and simmer for another 15–20 minutes.

You can also wrap gluten around rounds of *daikon* and deep-fry. Then place in water, *tamari* and *kombu* as above. Add thin rounds of lotus root and slices of onion and cook 30 to 45 minutes. Thicken *tamari* water with starch water and cook for another 15 to 20 minutes. Garnish with sprigs of parsley or sliced scallions, or chives. As another variation, wrap cauliflower or onions inside the gluten. Diced celery and mushrooms can be added to the sauce.

Noodles

I use several varieties of noodles which are made from different flours. For example, whole wheat noodles are available in a variety of shapes and sizes, and there are several kinds of buckwheat noodles, or *soba*, which vary in the proportion of buckwheat to whole wheat flour. Also, there is a delicious buckwheat noodle made from a combination of buckwheat flour and *jinenjo* (Japanese mountain potato) flour. Any whole grain noodle may be used in soups, salads, fried with vegetables, or boiled and served with a little *tamari* or with *tamari* broth.

To cook *soba*, first bring a pot of water to a boil (no salt should be added as the *soba* already contains salt). Add the noodles, turn the flame to medium-low and boil. To tell when they are ready, take one noodle out of the water and break off an end. If the inside is the same color as the outside, it is done. It needs more cooking if the inside is still white. When the noodles are done, remove from the pot and place in a strainer and rinse by running cold water over them. This will prevent the noodles from sticking together and keep them from cooking further. You may also eat them directly from the pot without washing.

Whole wheat noodles should be cooked in the same manner as above, except a small pinch of salt should be added to the cooking water before adding the noodles, as the whole wheat noodles contain no salt, and the salt helps them to cook properly.

Fried Noodles

1 package noodles
1 Tbsp. sesame oil
1/2 cup sliced scallions

1 cup sliced Chinese cabbage
1–2 Tbsp. tamari

Cook noodles as above, wash under cold water and allow them to drain for several minutes. Add oil to the skillet and heat. Add vegetables. Sauté vegetables for 5 minutes. Add noodles on top of vegetables. Cover skillet and cook on a low flame for several minutes, until the vegetables are done. (Some combinations of vegetables will take longer to cook than the combination I have given.) Add *tamari* to taste and cook for another 3–5 minutes. Mix noodles and vegetables near the end of cooking. This will keep the noodles from burning and allow the vegetables to cook faster and better. Make sure to keep the flame fairly low to avoid burning. Serve hot or cold.

As a variation, you can use onions and cabbage, scallions and carrots, *daikon* and *daikon* greens, celery and onions, scallions, Chinese cabbage and *tofu*, scallions and mushrooms, or other vegetable combinations. Please experiment.

Noodles and Broth

one 3-inch piece of kombu seaweed
4 cups water
2 dried mushrooms (shiitake)
2–3 Tbsp. tamari (should not be overly salty)

Cook noodles, wash, and drain. Place *kombu* in a pot and add water. Add *shiitake*. Bring to a boil. Reduce flame to medium-low and simmer for 3–5 minutes. Remove *kombu* and *shiitake*. (You may slice the *kombu* and *shiitake* into small pieces and add again to the soup or use them in something else.) Add *tamari* to taste and simmer for 3–5 minutes. Place noodles in the pot of hot broth to warm them up. Do not boil them again. Serve immediately. Garnish with slices of *shiitake*, scallion, and 1-inch squares of *nori*.

Recipes for various kinds of clear broth to use with noodles are given in the soup section on clear broth soups.

Noodle water may be saved and used as a beverage, for a soup stock, or in making bread. Slightly soured noodle water will help unyeasted bread to rise and makes an excellent sourdough bread starter.

Beans including *Tofu* and *Natto*

Beans are very high in protein, carbohydrate, iron, vitamins, and minerals, as illustrated in the chart on the next page.

Pressure-cooking is one of several ways to cook beans. When using this method use approximately three cups of water for each cup of beans. Wash beans as described earlier and place in pressure-cooker. Add water, cover, and place on flame. When the pressure comes up, reduce flame to medium-low and cook for approximately 45 minutes. Remove from flame and run cold water over the pressure-cooker. This will quickly bring the pressure down. Remove cover, add approximately 1/4 teaspoon of salt, and cook uncovered until the liquid evaporates.

	Protein	Carbo-hydrates	Iron	Vitamin A	Vitamin B
Azuki	21.5 gr	58.4 gr	4.8 mg	6 I.U.	2.5 mg
Lentils	24.7 gr	60.1 gr	6.8 mg	60 I.U.	2.0 mg
Chickpeas	20.5 gr	61.1 gr	6.9 mg	6.9 I.U.	2.0 mg
Pinto	22.9 gr	63.7 gr	6.4 mg		2.2 mg
Natto	16.9 gr	11.5 gr	3.7 mg		1.1 mg
Soybeans	34.1 gr	33.5 gr	8.4 mg	80 I.U.	2.2 mg
Black Beans	22.9 gr		7.9 mg		2.2 mg

(Information from U.S. Department of Agriculture and the Japan Nutritionists Association. From *The Book of Macrobiotics* by Michio Kushi. Measurements are per 100 grams.)

Another method is boiling. Place one cup of beans in a pot and add 3-1/2 to 4 cups of water. Bring to a boil, cover, and reduce flame to medium-low. Cook for approximately 1 hour and 45 minutes, depending on the type of bean, or until the beans are about 80% cooked. Add salt and cook for 15–20 minutes longer or until the liquid has evaporated.

A third way of cooking beans is by the "shocking" method. Place one cup of beans in a pot and add only enough water to lightly cover them. As the beans begin to cook they will absorb the water and expand. When this happens, add just enough cold water to again lightly cover the surface of the beans. Repeat this process until the beans are approximately 80% cooked (about 2 hours), add 1/4 teaspoon of salt and cook until water evaporates (about 15–20 minutes).

When adding cold water to the beans, slowly pour it down the side of the pot, rather than into the center, which would create too much of a shock. This allows the beans to slowly adjust to the temperature difference, while causing them to expand and then contract. In this way they will cook faster than by simply boiling.

A variation is to lay a strip of *kombu* seaweed on the bottom of the pot or pressure-cooker and place the beans on top. Then cook as for the three methods mentioned above. *Kombu* aids in the digestion of beans and prevents them from becoming soft and mushy while cooking. It also adds a slightly different flavor to the beans, and cuts down the cooking time.

Many people complain that beans are difficult to digest. If prepared and eaten properly, digestibility is no problem. The amount of water, salt and cooking time are the factors to be concerned with. As with all foods, beans should be chewed thoroughly for proper digestion and it is recommended that only a side dish of beans should be eaten at a meal.

Azuki Beans

1 cup azuki beans

water
1/4–1/2 tsp. sea salt

Wash beans and place in pot. Add just enough water to cover the surface of the beans. As the beans expand and absorb the liquid, add enough cold water to lightly cover them again. Cover and repeat this process until the beans are about 80% cooked (approximately 1-1/4 hours), then add salt and cook approximately 20 minutes longer. Remove cover and turn flame higher, and let the water evaporate. The entire cooking time should be about 2 hours.

For variety, add several pieces of cubed buttercup squash or Hokkaido pumpkin to the beans as you start to cook.

Lentils

These are the quickest of all the beans to cook. After washing, place one cup of lentils in a pot. Cover with water and cook for 45 minutes to one hour. Add additional water as needed. During the last 15–20 minutes of cooking, add approximately 1/4 teaspoon of sea salt. Remove cover and allow water to boil off.

Chickpeas

Wash beans and soak overnight. Place beans and soaking water in pressure-cooker and add enough additional water to equal 3 cups for each cup of chickpeas. Bring to pressure, reduce flame to medium-low and cook for 1 to 1-1/2 hours. Remove from flame and allow pressure to come down. After removing top, return pressure-cooker to burner and add 1/4 teaspoon of sea salt. Cook 45 minutes to 1 hour more.

As a variation, place a 3-inch strip of *kombu* seaweed on the bottom of the pressure-cooker and cook as above. After bringing pressure down, remove cover and add 1 small diced onion and 1 small quartered or diced carrot. Add sea salt and cook 45 minutes to 1 hour more.

Pinto Beans

Wash beans. Place one 3-inch strip of *kombu* on bottom of pot and layer the beans on top. Add enough water to just cover the surface of the beans. Place a lid that is smaller than the pot inside, so that it rests directly on the beans. (This keeps the beans from jumping up and down in the pot and will help them to cook faster.) If you don't add *kombu* your beans will become very soft. As beans expand add enough cold water to cover. Repeat until about 80% cooked. Then add salt (approximately 1/4 teaspoon per cup of beans) and cook until done. At this point, remove cover and cook until water evaporates.

As a variation, add diced carrots and onion during the last 1/2 hour of cooking.

Kidney Beans

Cook in the same manner as pinto beans. You can add 1-1/2 to 2 teaspoons of puréed brown rice *miso* per cup of beans, instead of sea salt, during the last 20 minutes for a different taste. When using *miso*, simply spoon it onto the top of the beans and cover with a lid. Do not mix until the beans are completely cooked. This gives the beans a mild, rich, delicious flavor, and a creamier texture.

Japanese Black Beans (or Black Soybeans)

Wash beans quickly and soak in water overnight, adding approximately 1/2 teaspoon of sea salt per cup of beans. Place beans in a pot. (Never pressure-cook black beans as they will clog the gauge on the pressure-cooker.) Add soaking water to the beans but do not add any more salt. Bring to a boil, then reduce flame to simmering point. Skim and discard the gray foam that floats to the top as the beans cook. When foam no longer appears, cover pot and cook for at least 2-1/2 to 3 hours. At the very end of cooking, add a small amount of *tamari* to make the skin of the beans shiny. Soaking in salt water prevents the skin of the beans from coming off during cooking. At the end of cooking, mix the beans and the juice by shaking the pot up and down several times.

These beans are therapeutic for the sexual organs and will relieve an overly yang condition caused by too much animal food or fish.

Soybeans

These beans are the most yin of the bean family. They are high in protein and oil. It is recommended that soybeans be eaten only occasionally as a separate side dish. Because they are very yin they should be cooked with yang vegetables such as lotus root or burdock, for balance.

The best way to eat soybeans is in the form of *tofu, okara, natto, tempeh,* and, of course, *miso* and *tamari.* Recipes for making *tofu, okara,* and *natto* are given later in this book.

Unless they are fermented, soybeans are not easily digested so it is very important to chew them very well.

Roast beans in a dry skillet or soak them for several hours. Place *kombu* seaweed on the bottom of a pot, and add beans. Sauté diced lotus root and diced carrots and add to the beans. Cook as for boiled beans.

Tofu

Tofu is made from soybeans which have been crushed and cooked. It is very high in protein. It can be served boiled, baked, fried, deep fried, plain, in soups, with vegetables, or as a garnish for noodles and broth. *Tofu* is becoming increasingly popular in the Western diet. It is such a versatile food that I am sure you can find many delicious ways to serve it. Please experiment!

Homemade Tofu

> **3 cups soybeans**
> **4-1/2 tsp. nigari (special salt made from sea water)**

Soak beans overnight, strain, and discard soaking water. Grind beans in an electric blender. (This is one of the few times I suggest using and electric appliance.) Or, if you have time and patience, use a Foley hand food mill. Add beans to about 6 quarts of water and bring to a boil. Reduce flame to low and simmer for about 5 minutes. Stir constantly to avoid burning. Sprinkle cold water on beans to stop bubbling. Bring gently to a boil again. Sprinkle cold water on beans. Repeat once more. (Do not cover the beans as they will bubble over the top of the pot.) Place a cotton cloth or several layers of cheesecloth in a strainer and pour the liquid, called soy milk, through the strainer, into a bowl. Fold the corners of the cloth together to form a sack and squeeze out the remaining liquid. Save the pulp in the sack. This pulp is called *okara*.

Grind the *nigari* in a *suribachi* or blender. Place the liquid soy milk in a bowl and sprinkle the ground *nigari* over it. Gently make two deep strokes in the mixture with a wooden spoon and let sit for 10–15 minutes. The *tofu* liquid should start to curdle. Most natural food stores sell special wooden or stainless steel *tofu* boxes. You will need either one of these or a bamboo strainer or steamer. Line box with cheesecloth and gently spoon in *tofu* liquid (soy milk). Cover the top with a layer of cheesecloth. Place wooden lid on top of the box so that it rests on the cheesecloth and *tofu*. Place a small weight on the lid. Let stand for approximately 1 hour or until a cake is formed. Then carefully place the *tofu* in a dish of cold water for about 1/2 hour. Refrigerate until ready to use.

When storing *tofu* in the refrigerator, make sure to keep it covered with water, as it will spoil easily if exposed to warmth. *Tofu* will keep for several days in this way.

Okara

Okara is the soybean pulp which remains after the liquid has been squeezed from the *tofu*.

> **2 cups okara**
> **1 stalk burdock diced or in matchsticks**
> **1 medium carrot diced or in matchsticks**

1 medium onion diced
1–2 cups kombu stock
tamari to taste

Lightly brush a skillet with oil. Heat, and sauté vegetables for 3–5 minutes. Add *okara* and soup stock. Bring to a boil, reduce flame, and cover pan. Simmer for 20–30 minutes. Stir occasionally, and season with sea salt or *tamari*. Cook until most or all of the water has been absorbed or evaporated.

For a drier texture, use only 1/4–1/2 cup *kombu* stock, and cook only 10–15 minutes.

Tofu and Corn

1 cake tofu
2 ears fresh sweet corn (remove kernels from ears)
tamari to taste or salt (pinch)

Lightly brush skillet with oil, and sauté corn for several minutes. Break *tofu* into small pieces or cut into small cubes. Add *tofu* to corn and cover. Simmer until corn is done. Season with a small amount of *tamari* (mixture should not be brown or salty), or add a pinch of sea salt instead.

As a variation, sauté onions, corn and *tofu*, or onions, corn, cabbage and *tofu*.

Tofu, Onions and Watercress

1 large onion sliced into rounds
2 cakes tofu
1/4–1/2 tsp. grated ginger
1 bunch watercress
1–2 tsp. tamari

Slice onion into 1/4 inch thick rounds and place on bottom of a skillet. Cover with water. Bring to a boil. Recude flame and simmer until onions are almost done, which should take about 10–15 minutes. Slice *tofu* into 2-inch cubes and place on top of the onions. Sprinkle the grated ginger over the *tofu*. Cover and cook for 5 minutes. Add *tamari* and place watercress on top of the *tofu*, cover and cook for 1 more minute. Serve in the skillet that was used to cook the dish. No stirring or mixing is necessary during preparation or for serving.

As a variation, use broccoli, cauliflower, carrots, burdock, cabbage or other vegetables instead of watercress.

Dried Tofu

Gently squeeze the water out of the *tofu* by placing the *tofu* on a board and covering it with a towel. Place another board on top of the *tofu* and a light weight on top of the board. Prop the boards up so that they are slightly tilted to allow the water to drain off. Let stand for about 1 hour. Slice the *tofu* into 1/2-inch slices and put in the freezer or place outside in the snow overnight. Bring indoors and allow the *tofu* to thaw out. Freeze to store.

Soak and slice dried *tofu* as needed. It can be used in soups, plain, or cooked with vegetables.

Yuba

Yuba is dried soy milk. Soak soybeans overnight. Grind soybeans in a mill. Place ground soybeans in a pot and add water until liquid becomes milky. Bring to a boil. Remove from flame and strain the soybean pulp through a cheesecloth sack to separate the soy milk from the pulp. Bring the soy milk to the boiling point. Skim off the layers of soy milk skin that floats to the top. Dry the soy milk by simply leaving it out exposed to the air, or put it in the oven at a low temperature until it becomes brittle. Store in a plastic bag until you are ready to use it. This is very yin and should only be used occasionally in special dishes or for party or holiday dinners.

Vegetables and Dried Soy Milk

> 1 daikon cut into rounds
> 1 burdock sliced diagonally
> 1 lotus root section sliced into rounds
> 1 three-inch strip of kombu
> 5 shiitake mushrooms
> 1/2 to 1 cup dried soy milk
> tamari to taste

Place *kombu* on bottom of pot. Layer *daikon*, lotus root, burdock, mushrooms and dried soy milk. (Before using, break the dried soy milk into small pieces or soak and cut into small squares.) Add enough cold water to half cover the vegetables. Add a pinch of salt and cook for 30 minutes. Add *tamari* to taste and cook for 20 to 30 minutes more.

As a variation, you can substitute strips of deep fried *tofu* for the dried soy milk.

Ganmodoki (*Tofu* and *Jinenjo* Patties)

Squeeze the water out of the *tofu* by placing the *tofu* on a board in the same way you would for making dried *tofu*. Then place the *tofu* in a piece of cheese-cloth and squeeze remaining water out.

2 cakes tofu
1 small onion diced
1/2 cup grated jinenjo
1 small carrot cut in matchsticks
1 small stalk burdock cut in matchsticks

Grind *tofu* in a *suribachi*. Mix in onion, *jinenjo*, carrot and burdock, add a pinch of sea salt and mix. Form into patties. (You may also add very finely chopped *shiitake* mushroom or lotus root to the patty mixture.) Deep fry the patties until golden brown on one side. Turn over and deep fry the other side until brown. Serve with grated *daikon* and *tamari*.

For variety, wrap the patties in roasted strips of *nori*.

Natto

Natto is a fermented soybean product that is high in protein, calcium, iron and Vitamin B (Niacin). *Natto* aids in the digestion of food in the intestines, and I have also noticed that it makes the skin feel smooth and young.

Natto has an interesting odor that may take some time to get used to. My observation has been that if a person eats or has eaten much dairy food in the past, he is more likely to dislike *natto* than a person who does not eat dairy or has been macrobiotic for several years and has discharged much of his past dairy food intake. *Natto* is usually eaten in Japan with a little *tamari* or mixed in a bowl with rice. It can also be served on top of buckwheat noodles.

To make your own *natto*, wash 4 cups of organic soybeans, and soak them in water for 4 to 6 hours. Discard soaking water. Place the beans in a pressure-cooker and cover with water. Leave the lid off the pressure-cooker, and bring the beans to a boil. Reduce the flame to low and simmer until a white foam floats to the top. Skim and discard the foam along with any loose soybean skins that float to the top. Repeat this process until the foam stops forming. Then place the top on the pressure-cooker. Do not add salt. Bring to pressure. Reduce flame to very low. Place under the pressure-cooker, and cook for 30–45 minutes. Let the pressure come down by running cold water over the outside of the pressure-cooker. Remove cover and pour beans into a strainer to drain and cool. When the beans are cool, place them in a pot.

To begin fermentation, the beans need to be mixed with a special type of of bacteria that is processed in Japan. As an alternative, you can purchase a package of fermented *natto* at a Japanese food store and mix one 3-1/2 oz. package in with the cooked soybeans. After mixing, cover the pot with a tight fitting lid and place in the oven with a temperature of 102–104 degrees F., which is the approximate temperature of the oven when the pilot light is lit. *Natto* will not ferment properly if it is exposed to a temperature lower or higher than this. Keep the *natto* in the oven for 22–24 hours without uncovering the pot or opening the oven door. Remove from oven, place in plastic containers and store in the freezer. Freezing stops the fermentation process. The beans will continue to ferment until they are inedible if not frozen. The above quantity of soybeans will yield 12–13 containers of *natto*, each with about seven and one-half ounce containers of *natto*. When you wish to serve, remove individual packages, thaw, and serve as described above.

Soup including Stocks and *Miso* Soup

Soups are an important part of the macrobiotic way of eating. There are several general methods of preparing soups and thousands of variations. I would like to explain some of these.

Many cookbooks recommend sautéing all of the vegetables before making a soup. Of course, this method makes delicious soups, but sautéing is not always necessary. My own experience has shown me that this style of preparation can result in the intake of too much oil. Often, when people have problems with their liver and gall bladder, they cannot tolerate large quantities of oil. Sautéing can be used occasionaly, but is not recommended for daily use.

As an alternative, the vegetables can be cooked in the soup stock. When making a split pea soup, for example, add the sliced vegetables to the split peas at the beginning of cooking, and cook until the peas are soft and the soup becomes creamy. Add a pinch of salt at the beginning to keep the vegetables from becoming mushy and to bring out their sweetness. Towards the end add additional salt.

To make *miso* soup, add the vegetables and seaweed to boiling water. Lower the flame and simmer until done. Then reduce flame to very low and add puréed *miso*.

Mrs. Kushi teaches what she calls the "layering method." It can be used not only for preparing soups but for beans, seaweed, and vegetable dishes as well. I feel that this method is superior to all others. Since the vegetables are not mixed until they are done, and the soup is left to cook by itself with no strring or other interference, it becomes tasty and sweet, and instills a calm and peaceful vibration when eaten. When using the layering method, arrange the vegetables and grains in the bottom of the pot from the most yin (onions, etc.) to the most yang (grain). For example, place sliced or diced onions on the bottom, followed by a layer of carrots, and one of sliced burdock. Put your grain on top. Then, add just enough water to cover the grain. Do not mix or stir the soup until the end of cooking. If you want to include green vegetables such as celery or scallions, add them during the last 10 minutes of cooking so that they retain their bright green color. In this way, the soup cooks with as little interference as possible, thus allowing the ingredients to blend naturally according to yin and yang, and to maintain their peaceful and natural quality.

When the grain begins to expand and absorb the water, add just enough water to cover it again. Repeat this process until the grain is cooked. At the beginning, add just a small pinch of salt to bring out the sweetness of the vegetables and grain. When the carrots are done, add the remainder of the salt to season. Finally add water to obtain the desired thickness of the soup.

Water should be poured down the side of the pot so as not to disturb the grain and vegetables or cause the vegetables to float to the top. Also, when making a dish like millet soup, it is best to add salt instead of *tamari*. Millet soup has an appetizing, soft yellow color. *Tamari* will turn it a brownish color which is not as appealing. When the natural color of the soup is maintained it is easy to find a vegetable, bean, and seaweed dish to complement it, thus enhancing the beauty of the entire meal,

Grain Soups

Millet Soup

1/2 cup millet
1 carrot (diced or quartered)
1 onion (diced)
1 small burdock stalk (halved or quartered)
1/2 stalk of celery (halved and sliced diagonally)
1/4–1/2 tsp. salt

Wash millet. Place onions on bottom of pot, then layer in succession carrots, burdock, and millet. Do not mix. Add a pinch of salt and just enough water to cover the top of the millet. Turn flame high. Bring to a boil. Reduce flame to low and simmer. When the millet starts to expand by absorbing the water, add only enough water to lightly cover again. Repeat this process until the millet is soft and starts to become creamy. When millet is completely cooked, add 4 cups of water and the remaining salt. (For a thick soup add less water; for a thin soup add more.) Simmer for another 20–25 minutes. During the final 10 minutes, add celery or greens. Garnish with scallions, celery leaves, or a sprig of parsley.

This method can be used in preparing just about any grain, bean, or vegetable soup. As a variation, a delicious soup can be made with barley, mushrooms, onions, carrots and celery.

Rice and Pumpkin Soup

1 cup Hokkaido pumpkin (or buttercup squash cut into 1/4–1/2 inch chunks)
2 cups cooked rice
1/2 cup diced onion
5–6 cups water
1/4–1/2 tsp. sea salt

Place onions on bottom of pot. Add pumpkin and put the rice on top. Add water and a small pinch of salt. Bring to a boil. Reduce flame to low and simmer for 45 minutes to one hour. At this point, add salt to taste and cook for 15–20 minutes longer.

Barley/Lentil Soup

1/2 cup barley
1/4 cup lentils
1 onion diced
1 stalk of celery diced
5–7 fresh mushrooms sliced
5–6 cups water
1/4–1/2 tsp. sea salt

Wash barley and lentils. From bottom to top, layer the onions, barley and lentils. Add water and bring to a boil Reduce flame to low and simmer until barley is almost done. Add celery, mushrooms and salt. Cook for another 15–20 minutes.

For a variation, barley, kidney beans, onions, celery and mushrooms are delicious.

Cream of Corn Soup

2 ears fresh corn (cut kernels off the cob)
1 cup diced onion

1/4 cup diced celery
1/4–1/2 cup corn flour
4 cups water
1/4–1/2 tsp. sea salt

Remove corn from the cob with a knife. Boil corn cobs in 4 cups of water. Save the water for the soup. Brush pot with a small amount of sesame oil. Sauté onions and corn with a pinch of salt. Add corn flour to onions and corn, and mix so that the vegetables are coated with the flour. Gradually add water to the flour and vegetables, stirring gently but constantly to avoid lumping. Bring to a boil. Reduce flame to low and simmer 1/2 hour. Add celery and salt and cook 15–20 minutes longer. Garnish with scallions, parsley or a sprig of watercress.

As a variation, you may omit the corn flour and season with *tamari* instead of salt.

Rice Soup

2 cups cooked rice
3 shiitake mushrooms
1 three-inch piece of kombu
1/2 cup scallions
1/4 cup diced celery
4 cups water
1–2 Tbsp. tamari

Boil *shiitake* and *kombu* for 2–3 minutes in 4 cups of water. Remove mushrooms and *kombu* and slice into thin strips. Place them back into the water, add rice, and bring to a boil. Reduce flame to low and cook for 20–25 minutes. Now add scallions and celery and simmer for 10–15 minutes. Add *tamari* and simmer for 5–10 minutes more.

Bean Soups

Azuki Bean Soup

1 cup azuki beans
1 medium sliced onion
1/2 cup sliced carrot
4 cups water
1/4–1/2 tsp. sea salt
tamari to taste (optional)

Wash beans, place in pot and add water. Bring to a boil. Reduce flame and simmer until beans are 80% cooked (about 1-1/4 hours). Add onions and carrots and pinch of salt. Cook for 20–25 minutes more. Add remaining salt and cook an additional 10–15 minutes. Add *tamari* to taste at very end if you wish. Garnish with scallions or parsley.

Lentil Soup

  1 cup lentils
  1 medium diced onion
  1 diced carrot
  1 small stalk of burdock quartered
  1 Tbsp. chopped parsley
  4 cups water
  1/4–1/2 tsp. sea salt

Wash lentils. Layer onions, carrots, burdock and lentils in that order. Add water and a pinch of salt and bring to a boil. Reduce flame to low and cover. Simmer for 45 minutes. Add chopped parsley and remaining salt. Simmer 20 minutes more and serve.

If some of the water evaporates add a little more to make it your desired consistency.

Split Pea Soup

  1 cup split peas
  1 medium onion diced
  1 carrot quartered
  1/2 cup soaked wakame
  4–5 cups water
  1/4–1/2 tsp. sea salt

Cook this soup the same way as the lentil soup. Slice the *wakame* into small pieces. This soup should be creamy and may require a little more cooking than the lentils.

As a variation, you can add 1/4 cup diced *jinenjo* (Japanese mountain potato).

Kidney Bean Soup

  2 cups kidney beans (cooked) or 1 cup uncooked beans
  1 medium sliced onion
  1/2 cup fresh sweet corn
  1 carrot sliced on the diagonal
  5–6 cups water
  1/2 tsp. sea salt
  tamari to taste (optional)

If the beans are uncooked, cook them for 1-1/4 hours first, then add vegetables and salt. If cooked, layer onions, corn, carrots and beans in that order, in a pot. Add water and a pinch of salt. Bring to a boil. Reduce flame. Cover pot and simmer for 30–40 minutes. Add remaining salt and simmer for 15 minutes more. At the end you can add *tamari* to taste if desired.

As a variation, wholewheat elbow macaroni can be included in the above recipe. Another variation is to use kidney beans, onions and celery.

Black Bean Soup

These black beans, also called turtle beans, are different from the Japanese black beans. Turtle beans are smaller and look somtehing like a navy bean.

    1 cup black beans
    carrot sliced
    1 medium onion diced
    4 cups water
    1/4–1/2 tsp. sea salt

Place beans in a pressure-cooker with water and bring to pressure. Reduce flame to low and cook for 45 minutes to 1 hour. Bring pressure down. Remove cover. Place beans and water in another pot. Add onions and salt. Cover and simmer for 20 minutes. Add carrots and simmer for 10–15 minutes. If desired, add *tamari* to taste. Garnish with parsley or scallions. If you add the carrots too soon the bean juice will turn them black.

Chickpea Soup

    1 stalk burdock quartered
    1 cup chickpeas soaked overnight
    1 onion diced
    1 carrot diced
    1 three-inch strip of kombu
    4–5 cups water
    1/4–1/2 tsp. sea salt

Place *kombu*, chickpeas, and water in a pressure-cooker and bring to pressure. Reduce flame to low and pressure-cook for 1 to 1-1/2 hours. Bring pressure down. Place beans in another pot. Add onions, burdock, carrots and salt. Cook for 20–25 minutes longer. Garnish with scallions or parsley.

Vegetable Soups

Onion Soup

1 large onion sliced very thin
1 three-inch strip kombu
3–4 shiitake mushrooms (soak 10–15 minutes)
1/4 cup sliced celery
4 cups water
2–3 Tbsp. tamari

Bring *kombu*, *shiitake*, soaking water and 4 additional cups of water to a boil. Reduce flame to low and simmer 3–4 minutes. Remove *kombu* and *shiitake*. Slice each into matchstick size pieces and place back in water. Add onions and cover. Simmer 20–25 minutes. Add celery and *tamari* and simmer for another 10 minutes. Garnish with deep fried bread crumbs or scallions.

Squash Soup

1 large buttercup squash or medium Hokkaido pumpkin cubed
1 medium diced onion
4–5 cups water
1/2 tsp. sea salt

Remove skin from squash. (Save skin. It can be cut into matchsticks and *tempuraed*.) Cube squash and place in pot with water. Add pinch of salt. Bring to a boil. Cover and reduce flame to low. Simmer until squash is soft, about 10–15 minutes. Remove squash and purée in a Foley food mill. Place puréed squash in a pot, add diced onion and remaining salt. Bring to a boil. Reduce flame to low and cook for 20 minutes. Garnish with scallions or parsley. This soup should be rather thick and creamy.

Vegetable Soup

3 three-inch strips of kombu (soak for 10 minutes)
2 carrots cut in triangular shape
1 large onion halved then quartered
1 stalk of burdock sliced diagonally
4–5 cups water
pinch of sea salt
1–2 Tbsp. tamari

Cut *kombu* into 1-inch pieces. Place *kombu*, carrots, burdock and onions in water. Add soaking water from the *kombu* and a pinch of sea salt. Bring to a boil. Reduce flame to low and simmer until *kombu* is soft, approximately 45 minutes to 1 hour. Add *tamari* and simmer for 15–20 minutes.

Clear Broth Soups

Tofu Soup

   2 cakes of tofu cubed
   1 three-inch piece of kombu
   2 shiitake mushrooms
   1/4 cup sliced scallions
   4 cups water
   2–3 Tbsp. tamari

Place *kombu* and *shiitake* in 4 cups water and bring to a boil. Boil for 3–4 minutes. Remove *kombu* and *shiitake*. (You may use the *kombu* and *shiitake* in another soup or dry again for later use.) Add *tamari* and simmer for 10–15 minutes. Add *tofu* and simmer on low flame for 5–10 minutes. Place soup in soup bowls and garnish with scallions and *nori*.

Watercress Soup

   1 bunch watercress
   1 three-inch strip kombu
   4 cups water
   2–3 Tbsp. tamari

Make a soup broth by boiling the *kombu* as with the *tofu* soup. Wash watercress carefully. Just before serving add the watercress to the broth and simmer for 1 minute. Serve. Carrots cut into flower shapes and boiled for 2–3 minutes make an attractive garnish.

Stocks

Shiitake Mushroom Stock

Soak 5 or 6 *shiitake* mushrooms in water for several minutes. Add *shiitake* and soaking water to 1 or 2 quarts of water and bring to a boil. Boil for 5–10 minutes. Remove *shiitake* and either slice them and add to the soup or use again in another recipe. Remove the woody stems if you add them to a soup. *Kombu* also goes very well in this stock.

Dried Vegetable Stock

Dice vegetables or slice them into rounds. Thread or tie on a string and hang them in the sun to dry out. Vegetables become sweet as they dry. When they are about half-dried, add to water and boil. Remove from water and use the liquid for soup stock. If dried completely, vegetables can be stored in an air-tight container and saved for future use.

Fresh Vegetable Stock

Vegetable roots, stems, tops or leaves can be used for making soup stock. Boil them in a few quarts of water for 5–10 minutes, then remove and discard the vegetables. Use the stock for any vegetable, grain, or bean soup.

Grain Soup Stock

Roast the grain until it is golden brown and gives off a nutty fragrance. Boil for 5 minutes and remove grain from stock.

Kombu Stock (Kombu Dashi)

If *kombu* is dusty, wipe quickly with a wet sponge. Washing removes valuable mineral salts, so unless there is obvious dust, *kombu* should not be washed. Add *kombu* to cold water and boil for 3–5 minutes. Remove the seaweed and save for use in other dishes or dry it out and use again for soup stock.

Fish Stock

Boil fish heads, and bones or dried bonito flakes for several minutes. Remove fish from water.

Miso Soup

Miso is an important item in macrobiotic cooking. It aids in the digestion of food in the intestines because of the natural enzymes that it contains and is high in protein, calcium, iron, and vitamin B_1 (Niacin).

Although there are many varieties of *miso* the one used most often is *Mugi miso*, which is made principally from soybeans, barley and sea salt. Brown rice *miso* is made from brown rice, soybeans and sea salt. *Kome miso* contains white rice, soybeans, and sea salt. *Hatcho miso* is made from soybeans and sea salt and is aged for over three years. Most *miso* is fermented for at least 1-1/2 years.

Mugi miso can be used the year round. Brown rice *miso* is much lighter and therefore lends itself to summer use, or it can be mixed half and half with *Mugi miso*. Being one of the most yang *misos*, *Hatcho* is not used regularly in this climate. We use it primarily in making the condiment *Tekka*, or in preparing *Takuan* pickles, the recipe for which is given later in this book. There are many other types of *miso*, such as white *miso*, red *miso*, and *natto miso*. These can be used in either vegetable or fish soups.

Miso can be used as a base for soups, in sauces, in spreads and condiments. It can be added as a flavoring to beans, when making bread, or in such vegetable dishes as onions or cabbage. For a variety of ideas for using *miso*, please refer to *How to Cook with Miso* by Aveline Kushi, published by Japan Publications, Inc.

Miso soup is usually served once a day. A lighter soup is better at breakfast, while a slightly stronger taste is better if you take your *miso* soup at suppertime.

Basic Miso Soup

1 ounce dry wakame (approximately 1/2 cup soaked)
1 medium onion sliced in half moons
4 cups water
2–3 Tbsp. puréed miso

Wash *wakame* twice under cold water quickly, to remove any dirt, and soak for 3–5 minutes. When it has softened slice into 1-inch pieces, place onions and *wakame* in a pot and add water. Bring to a boil, reduce flame and simmer for approximately 20 minutes, or until the *wakame* and onions are soft. Reduce flame to very low so that the water is not boiling or bubbling. Purée the *miso* with 1/4 cup soup water. Add approximately 1/2 teaspoon of puréed *miso* to each cup of water. Stir gently to mix in with soup. Simmer for 3–5 minutes and serve.

When you boil *miso* the beneficial enzymes, which aid in digestion, are destroyed. If you are making a *miso* soup and wish to have the beneficial enzymes, do not boil it. When adding *miso* to bean or vegetable dishes for flavoring, it is necessary to boil or simmer.

As a variation, you can use *wakame*, onions, and *tofu*; *daikon* and *daikon* greens; *wakame*, onions and carrots; onions and squash; Chinese cabbage and carrots.

Keep your morning *miso* soup simple, by avoiding an excess of ingredients. It is better to start the day with an uncluttered dish and it is difficult to complement each ingredient's taste if too many vegetables are used. If desired, a greater variety can be used in an evening soup.

Quick Miso Soup

1 cup water
1/8–1/4 cup sliced scallions
half sheet of nori cut into 1-inch squares
1/2–1 tsp. miso

Bring water to a boil. Reduce flame to very low, add scallions, and *miso*. Simmer 1 minute. Garnish with *nori*.

Watercress Miso Soup

4 cups water
1 bunch watercress (cut stems in thirds)
2–3 tsp. miso

Bring water to a boil. Reduce flame to low. Place watercress in water, cook 1 minute. Turn flame off. Add *miso*. Garnish with scallions, chives, or *nori*.

Daikon and Sweet Rice Dumpling Soup

4 cups water
1 cup daikon cut into thin rectangles 1/4–1/3 inch wide
1/2 cup chopped daikon greens
2 Tbsp. puréed miso

Dumplings

1/2 cup sweet rice or brown rice flour
1/4 cup boiling water
small pinch of salt

Add *daikon* and greens to water and bring to a boil. Reduce flame, cover and simmer until 1/2 done. Mix flour and boiling water together with a fork. Place a heaping teaspoon of the mixture in your hand and form into a ball. With your thumb make a thumbprint slightly into the dumpling. Repeat until you have several dumplings. Place dumplings into water with *daikon* and greens and simmer until they float to the top. When vegetables and dumplings are done, reduce flame to very low, and add puréed *miso*. Simmer 1 or 2 minutes. May garnish with scallions, or *nori*.

This dumpling *miso* soup is very hardy and delicious on a cold winter morning. Because of the dumplings the soup becomes thick and creamy.

Chinese Cabbage and Tofu Miso Soup

4 cups water
1 cup sliced chinese cabbage
1 cake of tofu cut into 1/2 inch cubes
1 small carrot cut diagonally
2–3 tsp. miso

Bring water to boil. Reduce flame to medium. Add carrot and cabbage, and *tofu*. When carrots are done, reduce flame to very low. Add *miso*. Simmer 1 or 2 minutes. Garnish with *nori* or scallions.

Daikon and Wakame Miso Soup

    4 cups water
    1 cup daikon cut into thin rectangles
    1 cup sliced wakame
    1/4 cup sliced celery
    2–3 tsp. miso

Add *daikon*, celery and *wakame* to water. Bring to a boil, reduce flame and simmer until vegetables are done. Reduce flame to very low. Add *miso*. Simmer 2–3 minutes.

Seaweed

Seaweeds are an essential part of the macrobiotic way of eating. They can be used in an almost infinite number of ways in soups, salads, with vegetables, as a soup base, or by themselves. They aid in the digestion of beans when cooked along with them. Seaweeds can also be roasted over a flame or in the oven and ground into a powder in a *suribachi* for use as a condiment.

Since our sea salt contains no added iodine we rely on seaweeds in our cooking to obtain this element.

Seaweeds are very high in calcium, iron, vitamin A, Niacin, vitamin C, and protein, as we can see in the following chart.

	Calcium	Iron	Vitamin A	Niacin	Vitamin A	Protein
Arame	1,170 mg	12 mg	50 I.U.	2.6 mg	0	7.5 gr
Hiziki	1,400 mg	29 mg	150 I.U.	4.0 mg	0	5.6 gr
Wakame	1,300 mg	13 mg	140 I.U.	10.0 mg	15 mg	12.7 gr
Kombu	800 mg	—	430 I.U.	1.8 mg	11 mg	7.3 gr
Nori	260 mg	12 mg	11,000 I.U.	10.0 mg	20 mg	35.6 gr
Dulse	567 mg	6.3 mg	—	—	—	—
Agar-Agar (Kanten)	400 mg	5 mg	0	0	0	2.3 gr

(Information from U.S. Dept. of Agriculture and the Japan Nutritionists Association. From *The Book of Macrobiotics* by Michio Kushi. Measurement is per 100 grams.)

Arame

This is a mild tasting seaweed. If you are just beginning to include them in your diet, you may find that *arame* is the easiest of the seaweeds to eat. It is black and turns dark brown when cooked.

> **2 cups soaked arame (approximately 1-1/4 ounce dry weight)**
> **1 medium onion sliced**
> **1 carrot sliced in matchstick style**
> **1 tsp. sesame oil**
> **water**
> **3–4 Tbsp. tamari**

Wash *arame* quickly under cold water, either in a bowl or strainer. Discard the rinse water. Soak *arame* in cold water for 3–5 minutes. Place *arame* on chopping block and slice diagonally into 1-inch pieces, then slice diagonally again in the opposite direction so that your slices form X's. Place oil in skillet and heat. Layer the onions, carrots and then the *arame* in the skillet. Add soaking water to almost cover the *arame*. Do not mix vegetables and *arame* until the very end of cooking. Bring to a boil, reduce flame and cover. Simmer on a low flame for 45 minutes to 1 hour. Remove cover and add *tamari*. Cover again and cook 20 minutes longer. Remove cover, turn flame medium to high and boil off excess liquid. There should be just enough liquid to serve. Finally, mix vegetables and seaweed together and serve.

    As a variation, you can use lotus root instead of carrots, or in combination with carrots and onions. Strips of deep fried *tofu* are delicious when cooked with sliced onions and arame or *hijiki*.

Hijiki

This seaweed is stronger tasting than *arame* and has a different texture. Some types of *hijiki* need to be cooked longer than *arame* to become soft. Simply simmer until soft before adding *tamari*.

    Hijiki is cooked in the same manner as *arame* and you may use the same combination of vegetables.

Wakame

> **2 cups soaked wakame**
> **1 medium onion sliced**
> **soaking water**
> **2 tsp. tamari**

Wash the *wakame* quickly under cold water, then soak in cold water for 3–5 minutes. Slice *wakame* into 1-inch pieces. Place the onions in a pot and cover with *wakame*. Add enough of the soaking water to almost cover the seaweed. Bring to a boil, reduce flame to low and simmer for 30 minutes or until the *wakame* is soft. Some types of *wakame* take longer to cook than others. Adjust simmering time accordingly. Add 2 teaspoons of *tamari* to taste and cook for 10–15 minutes longer.

As a variation, you may add carrots cut in triangular shapes and cook as above.

Kombu

Kombu makes an excellent stock for clear broth or vegetable soups. It is also delicious when boiled or baked with carrots and onions. Adding a strip of *kombu* to beans will help them to cook faster, serve as a flavoring and makes the beans easier to digest.

Sometimes, when I am boiling plain carrots or *daikon*, I add a small strip of *kombu* to the bottom of the pot and place the vegetables on top, add a pinch of salt, and cover with water. I bring this to a boil, reduce flame to low, and simmer until the vegetables are soft. This makes the carrots or *daikon* much sweeter than just boiling them in plain water.

Boiling:
  1 carrot cut in triangular shapes
  one 12-inch strip of kombu
  1 onion halved then quartered
  water
  1 tsp. tamari

Soak the *kombu* for 3–5 minutes. Slice it in half, then slice it diagonally into 1-inch pieces. Place it in a pot. Add onions, then carrots, and then enough of the soaking water to half cover the vegetables. Bring to a boil. Reduce flame to low and simmer for 30 minutes. Add *tamari* and cook for 10 minutes longer.

Baked:
  2 carrots cut in triangular shapes
  2 onions halved then quartered
  1/2 head of cabbage sliced into 1/2 inch strips
  1 three-inch strip of kombu
  1/2 cup water
  pinch of sea salt

Place *kombu* in a baking dish. Arrange onions in one corner of the dish, carrots in the center, and cabbage at the other side, to prevent flavors from mixing. For a slightly different taste, you may mix them together. Place water in dish and sprinkle a pinch of sea salt over the vegetables. Cover and bake at 375 degrees F. for 30–40 minutes or until the vegetables are soft.

Shio Kombu

As its name implies, *shio* (salt) *kombu* is very salty and should be used only occasionally as a condiment rather than a main-dish vegetable.

Soak several strips of *kombu*. Slice the strips in half, then slice them diagonally into 1-inch pieces. Place in a pot and add enough *tamari* to cover. Bring to a boil. Reduce flame to low and simmer until the *kombu* is soft and the *tamari* has cooked down considerably. If you want a less salty *kombu*, dilute the *tamari* with an equal amount of water.

Nori

Nori contains the highest percentage of protein of all the seaweeds. I found that if I eat *nori* several times per week, my desire for fish diminishes. *Nori* can be used as a garnish for soups, noodles, salads, etc., and makes a nice addition to *miso* soups. It can be added to fried rice, beans or cooked in *tamari* for several minutes, and is used in making *sushi*. *Nori* can be used in many different ways.

Rice Ball

> **1 cup cooked brown rice (or 1 handful)**
> **1 sheet toasted nori**
> **1/2–1 umeboshi plum**

Roast the *nori* (shiny side up) over the burner by holding it 10–12 inches above the flame, and rotating it until the color changes from black to green (about 3–5 seconds). Fold *nori* in half and tear, then fold in half again so that you have 4 equal sized pieces of *nori* (about 3 inches square).

Wet your hands in a dish of water with a pinch of salt diluted in it. Place rice in your hands and form it into a ball, as you would a snowball, or into a triangle by cupping your hands into a V-shape. Pack the rice to form a solid ball or triangle. With your thumb, press a hole in the center, and place a small piece of *umeboshi* inside. Then, pack the ball again to close the hole. Cover the rice ball, one piece at a time, with the *nori*, so that it sticks. You may have to wet your hands occasionally to keep the rice and *nori* from sticking to them, but do not use too much water. The less water you use in making a rice ball the better it will taste and the longer it will keep. The *umeboshi* inside helps prevent the rice from spoiling if it isn't eaten immediately and also aids in the digestion of the rice and *nori*.

Rice balls make a delicious, convenient snack anytime, and are ideal for traveling or when you carry your lunch. When making a rice ball for children use less or no *umeboshi* depending on the age of the child. Many interesting conversations develop when you eat one of these rice balls in a public place.

Rice balls can be made without using *nori* by simply packing the rice into a ball. As a tasty variation, you can roll it in a few roasted sesame seeds. You may also place a small piece of pickle or vegetables, or fish inside the rice ball as a substiture for *umeboshi*.

Dulse

Dulse may be eaten dry, although it has a salty and strong taste. It can also be used in seasoning soups or soaked and sliced and added to salads. Dulse can be roasted and ground in a *suribachi* to make a condiment. It can also be used in making *miso* soups, or as a garnish for soups.

Agar-Agar

This seaweed has a white color and, when cooked, forms into a gelatinlike substance. It is used mainly in dessert cooking to make *kanten*, which is a fruit gelatin. It can also be used, however, to make a vegetable aspic or an aspic with *azuki* beans and raisins. Agar-agar is almost colorless and odorless. It comes prepackaged with preparation directions printed on the package. I will explain how to make *kanten* in the section on dessert cooking.

Vegetables and Salads

Vegetables

There are a variety of ways of preparing vegetables, each producing distinct flavors and textures. Sautéing, boiling, steaming, baking, pressure-cooking and deep frying (*tempura*) are the most widely used methods.

Sautéing

Sautéing is generally the most commonly used method in macrobiotic cooking. There are two types of sautéing, In the first, cut the vegetables into matchsticks, thin slices, or shave them. Brush a skillet with a small amount of light or dark sesame oil. Heat the oil. Add the vegetables and a pinch of sea salt to bring out their natural sweetness. Sauté the vegetables by occasionally moving them gently from side to side with chopsticks to ensure even cooking. You do not need to stir the vegetables. Sauté for 5 minutes on a medium flame. Reduce flame to low and sauté for another 10 minutes or so, gently mixing occasionally to avoid burning. Season to taste with sea salt or *tamari* and sauté 2–3 minutes longer and serve.

The second method uses water as well as oil. The vegetables can be cut into larger, thicker pieces or in the same size as for the above method. First, sauté the vegetables in a small amount of sesame oil over a medium flame for approximately 5 minutes. Then add enough water to almost half-cover the vegetables or lightly cover the surface of the skillet. Add a pinch of sea salt, cover, and cook until the vegetables are tender. Season with *tamari* or sea salt to taste near the end of cooking. Remove cover and simmer until remaining water is evaporated.

Sautéed Burdock and Carrots (Kinpira)

  1 cup shaved burdock
  1/2 cup shaved carrots
  1 Tbsp. sesame oil
  pinch of sea salt
  tamari to taste

Use the second method mentioned above except sauté the burdock for several minutes before adding the carrots, as the burdock takes longer to cook than the carrots.

Other Variations—using either the first or second method
  Carrots and onions
  Cabbage, carrots and onions
  Yellow summer squash and onions
  Celery and mushrooms
  Kale
  Kale and carrots
  Kale and *seitan*
  Brussels sprouts
  Parsnips and onions
  Parsnips, onions, and carrots
  Chinese cabbage, mushrooms, and *tofu*
  Broccoli
  Broccoli and cauliflower
  Snowpeas, scallions, mushrooms, and celery
  Chinese cabbage, celery and mung bean sprouts
  Cabbage and *seitan*
  Swiss chard and *tofu*
  Onions and *tofu*
  Corn and onions
  Corn, onions and *tofu*
  Cabbage, corn, onions and *tofu*

There are infinite combinations you can use.

Boiling

There are two methods. The first is to place vegetables in cold water and add a pinch of salt. Bring to a boil. Reduce flame to medium-low and simmer until vegetables are tender but slightly crisp.

I use the second method mainly for carrots or *daikon*. Place a 3-inch strip of *kombu* on the bottom of a pot, add the vegetable or vegetables and sprinkle a pinch of salt over them. Bring to a boil. Reduce the flame and simmer until done. Your carrots and *daikon* will taste very sweet with this method.

Tamari can be used instead of salt to season vegetables. For instance, place a strip of *kombu* on the bottom of a pot. Layer quartered onions, *shiitake* mushrooms, *daikon* sliced into rounds, lotus root sliced into rounds, and finally burdock. You may also add several strips of deep fried *tofu* at the very end of cooking. Add water to half-cover the vegetables and a pinch of salt. Bring to a boil. Reduce flame to low and simmer for about 1 hour or until the lotus root and burdock are tender. Add *tamari* to taste the last 10–15 minutes of cooking.

Instead of layering the vegetables you can place quartered onions, carrots cut into triangles, several *shiitake* mushrooms, *daikon* cut into rounds, and several pieces of *seitan* in the bottom of the pan. Arrange the vegetables so that each has its own area in the pot, making sure it is not mixed with the other vegetables. Add a pinch of salt and enough water to half-cover the vegetables. Bring to a boil, reduce the flame and simmer for about 45 minutes to 1 hour. Add *tamari* to taste the last 10–15 minutes of cooking.

By using an attractive pot to cook the vegetable in this way you can serve directly from the pot at the table rather than placing in a bowl. If you choose to serve from a bowl, arrange the vegetables in the same way they were cooked in the pot to create an attractive dish.

When you are boiling or steaming vegetables do not overcook them. They are hot when you take them from the pot and tend to continue cooking slighly from the heat they have absorbed. Wait until the vegetables have cooled before covering their serving dish with a bamboo mat, or they will turn a dull color. If you want to keep the vegetables a very bright color, and stop the cooking process after you remove from the cooking pot, simply place the vegetables in a strainer and run cold water over them.

You may also season boiled vegetable dishes with *miso* instead of *tamari* or sea salt. For example: onions and *miso*; onions, carrots and *miso*; cabbage, onions, carrots and *miso*; *daikon* and *miso*; *daikon*, onions and *miso*; *daikon*, Chinese cabbage and *miso*; etc. Add just enough *miso* to bring out the sweetness of the vegetables. It should not be salty.

Steaming

There are two basic methods of steaming vegetables. With the first, put about 1/2 inch of water in the pot. Insert a vegetable steamer inside the pot, or, if you have a Japanese wooden steamer, place it on top of the pot. Place the vegetables in the steamer and sprinkle with a pinch of salt. Cover and bring the water to a boil. Steam until tender. (Approximately 5–7 minutes depending on the size and thickness of the vegetables.)

The second method can be used if you don't have a vegetable steamer. Place 1/4 inch of water in the bottom of a pot. Add the vegetables and sprinkle with a pinch of salt. Bring to a boil. Lower flame to medium and steam until done. (Steamed or boiled vegetables should be slightly crisp but not raw.)

Save the vegetable water from the boiled or steamed vegetables for use as a soup stock, or base for a bechamel or *kuzu* sauce.

Baking

There are several ways to bake vegetables. For instance, when baking summer squash, first remove the stem, and then cut the squash in half. Using a knife, make diagonal slashes in the skin of the squash, then make diagonal slashes in the opposite direction, thus creating **X**'s on the surface of the skin. With a vegetable peeler or knife, make a hollow hole for an eye. Also, make thin slices in the neck to create a tail. (See diagram.) Place the squash on an oiled baking pan or cookie sheet. Lightly brush the top of the squash with sesame oil if desired or, if you are reducing your oil intake, omit this step. Bake the squash at 375 degrees F. for about 20 minutes. Then pour a couple of drops of *tamari* on top of each piece and bake for 15–20 minutes longer or until the squash is done. Your squash will resemble a baked fish when prepared in this way.

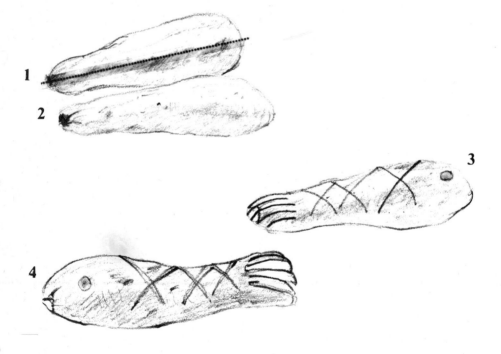

Butternut, buttercup, Hokkaido pumpkin, acorn, and Hubbard squash require more time to bake. Brush a baking pan or cookie sheet lightly with oil. Cut the squash in half and clean out the seeds. Place on the baking pan with the skin side up and bake at 375–400 degrees F. for 1–2 hours or until done. The squash can be seasoned by rubbing a pinch of salt on its inside before cooking, or by adding a little *tamari* at the end, but this is not necessary. Turn the halved squash upside down during the final ten minutes of cooking to let some of the liquid evaporate. A delicious variation is to stuff the halved squash with rice and vegetables or bread crumbs, onions, celery, and *seitan*. In this case, use a covered baking dish to help the rice and vegetables cook and then, during the last 10–15 minutes, remove the cover to allow the liquid to evaporate.

You may also either bake the squash whole, or stuff a whole squash and then bake. First cut a circular hole in the top of the squash and clean out the seeds. Season with salt or stuff the squash and bake until done. The baking time will differ depending on the size and type of squash.

Poke the squash with a chopstick or fork to see if it is done. If it goes through easily the squash is ready, but if it is still hard, bake it longer.

There are three ways to bake root or green vegetables. One is to place *kombu* in a baking dish, then place the vegetables on top. Add 1/4–1/2 inch of water to the baking dish and bake at 375–400 degrees F. for 30–45 minutes or until done. Another method is to omit the *kombu* and bake as above. A third way is to brush the baking dish lightly with sesame oil, place the vegetables in the pan, sprinkle with salt and bake as above. When preparing vegetables in this manner, cover the baking dish to lock in the natural juices and to prevent the vegetables from drying out through evaporation.

Another method of baking vegetables is to make a pastry dough, roll it out as you would for a pie and wrap such partially-boiled vegetables as whole carrots or burdock in it. Bake at 375 degrees F. until the crust is golden brown or the vegetables are tender. Then slice the roll into rounds and serve.

Arame or *hijiki* rolls can be made in the same manner by wrapping the seaweed in pastry dough and baking as above. Cut into rounds and serve.

You can also make a vegetable or seaweed pie in the same way as you would for a fruit pie simply by substituting seaweed and vegetables for the fruit.

Broiling

Place vegetables such as onions, broccoli, cauliflower, mushrooms, carrots and *seitan* on a shishkebab skewer or bamboo stick. Occasionally baste vegetables with a mixture of water, sesame oil and *tamari* or the vegetables will dry out. Cook under the broiler until done. This only takes several minutes. Fish can be used instead of *seitan*. If you use fish, first marinate it in *tamari* and ginger, then broil it on a skewer.

Sukiyaki

Sukiyaki is a one-dish meal that is cooked and served in the same cast iron skillet. It can include a variety of different vegetables, noodles, *seitan* or fish, cooked in water and *tamari*. I have found the following *sukiyaki* dish to be very delicious.

> **1 medium onion halved then quartered or cut into rounds**
> **1 bunch of watercress**
> **4–6 broccoli flowerettes**
> **1 carrot sliced diagonally**
> **1/4 head of cabbage cut in quarters**
> **5–6 slices buttercup squash**
> **1 cake tofu cut into 1-inch cubes**
> **5–6 fresh mushrooms**

When making *sukiyaki*, the vegetables that require the longest cooking time are added to the skillet first. With the above recipe you would place the onions, broccoli, carrots, cabbage, squash, and mushrooms in the skillet so that each vegetable has its own separate place and is not mixed with the others. Arrange the vegetables so that the colors are balanced and attractive. Do not, for example, place the squash and carrots next to each other as they are similar in color. Instead, put the broccoli or cabbage next to the squash, the onions in the center and the carrots on the opposite side for contrast. Add enough water to cover the bottom of the skillet. Sprinkle with a pinch of salt. Cover the skillet and bring to a boil. Reduce flame to low and simmer until the vegetables are almost done. Add *tamari* to taste but it should not be salty. Cover and cook for 2–3 minutes. Then add the *tofu* and cook for 2–3 minutes. Add watercress and cook 1 minute. The *tofu* and watercress are added at the end of cooking because they require less cooking time than the other vegetables. Serve hot in the skillet with a dip sauce of *tamari* and ginger, or a thin *tofu* sauce.

As a variation you can use *seitan*, carrots, *daikon*, escarole, onions, scallions, *shiitake* mushrooms, noodles and celery.

There are many different combinations you can use in this dish. Just remember to add the vegetables that require the longest cooking time first and the quicker cooking vegetables toward the end. Please experiment with different combinations.

Tempura

Vegetables that are dipped in batter and deep fried are known as *tempura*. Sesame oil is the best quality vegetable oil for making *tempura*. Never use corn oil in this way; it is very yin and will expand quickly and bubble all over your stove. Fill a 10- or 12-inch cast iron skillet or Dutch oven with at least 2–3 inches of sesame oil. Heat the oil to about 350 degrees F. but don't let the oil smoke. To test for the right temperature, drop a small morsel of batter into the hot oil. If the oil is ready, it should sink to the bottom of the skillet and almost immediately rise to the surface. Dip the vegetables one at a time in batter and drop gently into the oil. Do not add too many pieces to the skillet at one time. When one side becomes golden brown, turn each piece with chopsticks or a wire strainer and brown the other side. Remove the vegetables from the skillet and drain excess oil by placing on a wire *tempura* rack or on paper towels. To keep the vegetables crisp, place them on a cookie sheet in a warm oven (200 degrees F.). Serve hot.

Tempura Batter No. 1
  3/4 cup wholewheat pastry flour
  1/4 cup corn flour (or sweet rice flour)
  1 to 1-1/4 cups water
  1/4 tsp. sea salt

Tempura Batter No. 2
  1 cup wholewheat pastry flour
  1 to 1-1/4 cups water
  1/4 tsp. sea salt
  2 level tsp. arrowroot or kuzu

Mix dry ingredients. Then add water and stir until batter is smooth. Some of the batter will separate from the dipped vegetables when they are added to the hot oil. Your batter is too thin if it separates too much. In this case simply add a little more flour. If none of the batter separates, it is probably too heavy. Just add a little more water. It is best to prepare your batter ahead of time, so it can sit a few minutes before using. Keep it in a cool place. If the batter is exposed to warm air it may become a little thick. If so, just add a little water to regain desired consistency.

Hundreds of different vegetables, and even apple slices, can be *tempuraed*. You can use carrots, cauliflower, broccoli, brussels sprouts, mushrooms, lotus root, kale, dandelion leaves and roots, parsley, carrot tops, squash, celery, celery leaves, green and yellow string beans, onions, burdock, *tofu* and many others. If the vegetables are wet, dry them off with a towel before dipping them into the batter. You can also cut vegetables into matchsticks or dice them, and add them directly to the batter. Put spoonfuls of the vegetable batter into the hot oil and *tempura*.

Tofu should be drained of excess water before deep frying. To do this, place the *tofu* on a board, place another board on top of the *tofu* and a bowl on top of the board to squeeze out the water. The board should be placed on a slight angle or tilt to allow the excess water to run off. The pressure on the top of the *tofu* should not be too heavy or it will squash the *tofu*. After the water is drained off, slice or cube the *tofu*, dip it in batter and fry or deep fry it with or without batter.

Seafood such as shrimp, haddock, sole, squid, clams, oysters, smelt and others are delicious when *tempuraed* in basically the same manner. For instructions on fish *tempura*, please refer to the section in this book describing the preparation of fish.

Clean your oil by skimming it with an oil skimmer to remove chunks of batter debris. To remove odors, drop an *umeboshi* plum into the hot oil and deep fry it until it chars. If you have previously *tempuraed* fish, for instance, you will want to remove the fish odor from the oil before you *tempura* vegetables. Your *tempura* oil can be stored in a glass jar or in your *tempura* pot. It should be tightly covered and kept in a dark or shaded place. It will remain good for two to three months. Add new oil as needed. You should always have about 2 or 3 inches of oil in your *tempura* pot.

Tempura should be served with a sauce made of grated *daikon* or ginger and *tamari* to help digest the oil.

Daikon Sauce	Ginger Sauce
1/4 tsp. grated daikon	1/8 tsp. grated ginger
1 Tbsp. tamari	1 Tbsp. tamari
1 Tbsp. water	1 Tbsp. water

Mix ingredients and serve in small cup or bowl. Each person should have one dish of the mixture to dip the *tempura* in.

You may also serve plain grated *daikon* (about a tablespoonful with a drop of *tamari* poured on it to each person), instead of, or in addition to, the dip sauce.

Aveline Kushi's Miso Stuffed Lotus Root

1 section lotus root (fresh)
2 Tbsp. tahini
1 Tbsp. miso
1/4–1/2 tsp. grated ginger
1–2 tsp. minced parsley
1/4 cup wholewheat flour

Wash lotus root and cut off ends. Boil whole lotus root in water for 5–10 minutes. Combine *tahini, miso*, ginger and parsley in a bowl and mix. Gently pound one of the open ends of the lotus root into the bowl of *miso* mixture. As you pound the *miso* will fill the lotus chambers. When the chambers are full of the *miso* mixture from one end to the other, place the lotus in a dish and let sit for 1 hour. The *miso* will draw liquid out of the lotus root. Roll the lotus in this liquid. Then roll the lotus in wholewheat flour. Place whole lotus into *tempura* batter and deep fry for 2 or 3 minutes or until golden brown on the outside. Drain and cool. Cut into thin rounds and arrange attractively on a platter. This is very yang and each person should only have one or two slices.

Pressure Cooking

Pressure-cooked vegetables are very delicious because none of the juice or vitamins, etc. can escape. Cooking vegetables in this manner requires a very short cooking time and much less water than boiling. To pressure-cook vegetables simply slice vegetables into desired size, place in pressure-cooker. Add water and a pinch of salt. Bring to pressure, reduce flame, simmer several minutes depending on the size and type of vegetable. Remove from flame, bring pressure down and place in a serving dish.

More yin vegetables or thinly sliced vegetables only require approximately 1–5 minutes and 1/2–1 cup water. More yang or large chunks of vegetables require 5–8 minutes and 1/2–1 cup water.

Vegetable	Time
Broccoli	2–3 minutes
Brussels sprouts	4–5 minutes
Burdock	15–20 minutes
Cabbage—large pieces	6–8 minutes
small pieces	2–3 minutes
Carrots—slices	2–3 minutes
whole	4–5 minutes
Cauliflower	3–4 minutes
Celery	1–2 minutes
Corn—cob	1–2 minutes
kernels	1–2 minutes
Daikon	3–5 minutes
Green beans	2–3 minutes
Kale	1–3 minutes
Onions—whole	6–8 minutes
quartered	1–2 minutes
Squash	5–7 minutes

Save the cooking water for soup stock or for sauces.

Example:

1 daikon sliced into rounds or halved
4 stalks burdock (1/4–1/2 inch chunks)
3 pieces of kombu 12 inches long
1 Tbsp. tamari
1-1/2 to 2 cups water

Soak *kombu*, then slice into 1/2 inch strips. Place on bottom of pressure-cooker.

Place *daikon* on top of *kombu*. Place burdock on top of *daikon*. Add 1-1/2 to 2 cups *kombu* soaking water and 1 tablespoon *tamari*. Bring to pressure, reduce flame to low and simmer for 15–20 minutes. Remove from flame and bring pressure down. Place in serving bowl.

As a variation you may add *shiitake*, lotus root, or deep fried *tofu* to this dish also.

Salads

Salads are simple to make and are very good in hot weather or to balance a yang meal. Examples of the many types of salads are bean salads, raw salads, boiled salads, pressed salads, noodle salads, seaweed salads, and fruit salads.

Bean Salad

  1 cup cooked kidney beans
  2 cups steamed green string beans
  1 cup steamed wax beans (yellow)

Combine beans and serve with *umeboshi* or scallion-parsley dressing. (Preparation of dressings is explained shortly.) Serve cool in summer.

Chickpea Salad

  1 cup cooked chickpeas
  1/2 head lettuce
  1/2 shredded carrot

Combine ingredients and serve with *umeboshi*, scallion-parsley dressing, tahini dressing or *tofu* dressing.

Boiled Salad

  1 cup sliced Chinese cabbage
  1/2 cup carrots cut in matchsticks
  1/2 cup sliced celery
  1/2 cup sliced onion
  1 bunch watercress

When making a boiled salad, boil each vegetable separately. All of your vegetables, however, may be boiled in the same water. Cook the mildest tasting vegetables first, so that each will retain its distinctive flavor. For example, Chinese cabbage is the mildest tasting of the above vegetables. Drop into 1 inch boiling water in which a pinch of salt has been added. This will help the vegetables retain their bright color and accent their natural sweetness. Boil for 1–2 minutes, depending on the thickness of the vegetable. All of the vegetables should be slightly crisp but not raw. Next boil the onions, then the carrots, celery, and last the watercress, as it has a very strong taste. Watercress only needs to be boiled for a few seconds. Place vegetables one at a time in a strainer and run cold water over them to keep their bright colors. Mix vegetables together. Serve with *tofu* dressing or mix the *tofu* dressing in with the vegetables just before serving.

Noodle Salad

2 cups of wholewheat shells, elbows or alphabet noodles
1/2 cup shredded carrot
1 sliced cucumber
1 stalk celery sliced
1 diced onion

Cook noodles, wash and drain. Mix noodles with raw or partially boiled vegetables. Mix with *tahini* or *umeboshi* dressing.

Hijiki Salad

Boil *hijiki* in plain water for 35–45 minutes. Remove, drain and slice. Place on top of raw salad and serve with *tofu* dressing.

Fruit Salad

1 sliced apple
1/4 cup raisins
1 cup canteloupe (cubed or shaped in balls with a melon spoon)
1 cup watermelon (cubed or shaped in balls with a melon spoon)
1/2 cup green grapes
pinch of sea salt

Mix and serve on a warm summer day.

Dressings, Spreads, Sauces and Dips

Dressings

Tofu Dressing

 1 cake of tofu
 1/2 tsp. puréed umeboshi plum
 1/4 grated or diced small onion
 2 tsp. water (may use more water to make creamier)
 chopped scallions or parsley to garnish

Purée onion, *umeboshi*, and water in a *suribachi*. Add *tofu* and purée until creamy. Garnish with chopped scallions or sprigs of parsley and 5 slices of partially boiled carrots cut in flower shapes. Serve with boiled or raw salad.

Umeboshi Dressing

 2 umeboshi plums or 2 tsp. umeboshi paste
 1/2 tsp. sesame oil
 1/2 cup water (or more if desired)
 1/4–1/2 tsp. grated onion

Purée *umeboshi* and onion in *suribachi*. Heat oil. Add oil and purée. Add water and mix. Serve with raw, boiled, or noodle salad.

Scallion-Parsley Dressing

 1/4 cup sliced scallions
 1 Tbsp. chopped parsley
 1/2 tsp. sesame oil
 1 cup umeboshi juice (or 1 cup water and 2 umeboshi plums)

To make *umeboshi* juice, take 3–4 *umeboshi* plums and place in 1 cup of water. Place in a glass jar and shake water and plums. Let sit for 1/2 hour. Drain water from plums. Save plums; they can be used again.
   Place scallions, parsley, sesame oil and *umeboshi* juice in a jar and shake. Serve over raw, boiled or noodle salad.

Tahini Dressing

  2 umeboshi plums or 1/2 tsp. umeboshi paste
  2 Tbsp. tahini
  1/2 small diced or grated onion
  1/2–3/4 cup water

Purée onion, *umeboshi* and *tahini* in a *suribachi*. Add water and purée until creamy. Serve on raw, boiled, noodle or *hijiki* salad.

Spreads, Sauce and Dips

Miso-Tahini Spread

  6 Tbsp. tahini
  1 Tbsp. mugi or brown rice miso

Roast *tahini* in a dry skillet over a medium-low flame until golden brown. Stir constantly to avoid burning. Remove from burner and gently stir in *miso*. For a different flavor, add a few chopped scallions. This spread is delicious with whole-grain bread.

Miso-Sesame Spread

Prepare in the same way as *miso-tahini*, but substitute sesame butter for *tahini*.

Other Spreads

Spreads can be made from a variety of vegetables and fruits. Some combinations you might wish to try are: squash, onions and *miso*; squash and apples; apple butter; scallion or chives and *miso*; *tofu*, *umeboshi* and scallions; etc. Please experiment.

Bechamel Sauce

  1/2 cup wholewheat pastry flour or rice flour
  3 cups water or vegetable stock or kombu soup stock
  1 medium diced onion
  1 Tbsp. tamari

Brush skillet lightly with oil. Sauté onion until it becomes transparent. Add flour and toast for 2–3 minutes. Stir so that each piece of onion is coated with flour. Add water gradually and stir constantly to avoid lumping. Add *tamari*, cover, bring to a boil and then cook over a low flame for 10–15 minutes. Place an asbestos pad under the skillet to prevent burning. Stir occasionally to prevent sticking to the bottom of the skillet.

As a variation, add diced celery and mushrooms.

This sauce is very good when served over kasha, millet or *seitan*. However, sauces should be used only on occasion, since they tend to create mucus in the body if eaten regularly.

Kuzu Sauce

1-1/2 cups vegetable stock or water
1 Tbsp. kuzu

Dilute *kuzu* in a small amount of cold water and add to water or to vegetable stock. Bring to a boil, lower flame, and simmer for 10–15 minutes, stirring constantly. Add *tamari* to taste. Serve over vegetables or *tofu*, or add to a Chinese style vegetable dish made with bean sprouts, Chinese cabbage, onions, celery, and mushrooms.

Miso-Lemon Sauce

2 Tbsp. miso
6 tsp. lemon juice (or tangerine juice)

Mix ingredients until creamy. Serve on bread, toast or with vegetables as a condiment.

Chickpea Dip

2 cups chickpeas
1 small onion diced
2 umeboshi plums

Cook chickpeas as described in the section on beans. Purée onion and *umeboshi* in *suribachi*. Add to chickpeas. Purée mixture in a Foley food mill. Garnish with scallions or parsley. Serve with bread, corn chips, or crackers.

Tofu Dip

Use same recipe as for *Tofu* Dressing. Include chives or scallions to vary the taste. Serve on bread, with corn chips, or crackers.

Condiments and Garnishes

Condiments

Miso with Scallions

Miso is used primarily in soups, sauces or spreads, although it can be served occasionally as a condiment.

   1 cup chopped scallions
   1 Tbsp. miso
   1 Tbsp. water
   1 tsp. sesame oil

Sauté scallions in oil. Purée *miso* in *suribachi* with water. Add *miso* to scallions and gently mix. Place on low flame for 5–10 minutes. Serve with rice or noodles.

Tamari

Tamari is the name given to the soy sauce that is traditionally processed, without chemicals, sugar, or preservatives. It is a by-product of *miso*. I recommend that you use it mainly in cooking or in the preparation of medicinal foods, rather than as a condiment. If necessary, a small amount may be added at the table, to soups or noodles to enhance their flavor. It can also be used when eating *natto*. However, *tamari* should generally not be used on rice.

Umeboshi

Umeboshi is a variety of plum that has been pickled in sea salt. It helps establish the intestinal flora necessary for good digestion. *Umeboshi* may be used in rice balls, salad dressings, with vegetables, as a condiment served with rice, and in medicinal preparations.

Gomasio

Gomasio is made from roasted sesame seeds and sea salt. It may be sprinkled over rice, other grains, or vegetables. Sesame seeds are very high in protein, calcium, phosphorous, iron, vitamin A and Niacin. *Gomasio* provides an excellent way of taking in salt, as the salt is coated with oil which aids in its digestion. It should be used moderately, however. The recommended proportions for *gomasio* are one part sea salt to 8–14 parts sesame seeds. For children, use much less salt than this. *Gomasio* adds and slightly nutty flavor to your food.

The key to making delicious *gomasio* is good health and patience. It should not be made quickly. To store *gomasio*, place it in a jar and cover tightly. Try to make it fresh every week.

1 cup sesame seeds
1-1/3 Tbsp. sea salt

Wash sesame seeds. Roast in a dry skillet over a low flame. Stir continuously with a wooden spoon, shaking the skillet from time to time so that the seeds will roast evenly. When the seeds give off a nutty fragrance, darken in color, and begin popping, crush one between the thumb and index finger. If it crushes easily, it is done.

Pour seeds immediately into a *suribachi*. They will burn if left in the skillet after the flame has been turned off. Add salt. Slowly grind the seeds and salt with an even, circular motion until each seed is half crushed. *Gomasio* should not be too fine. Store in tightly sealed container.

Seaweed Powders

Seaweed powders can be made by roasting either dulse, *wakame* or *kombu* in an oven until they become dark and crisp, and then grinding them into a powder in a *suribachi*. Seaweed powders are rich in protein, calcium, iron, and minerals.

You may also roast sesame seeds and grind together with the seaweed to make a different condiment.

If you are anemic, make a condiment by grinding together roasted *kombu* and roasted *chirimen iriko* (small dried fish) into a powder. This is very high in calcium and iron. It can occasionally be sprinkled on your rice.

Tekka

1/4 cup sesame oil
1/3 cup finely minced burbock
1/3 cup finely minced carrot
1/3 cup finely minced lotus root
1/2 tsp. grated ginger
2/3 cup Hatcho miso

Mince the vegetables as finely as possible. Heat cast iron skillet, and add half of the oil. Heat oil. Sauté the burdock, carrot, lotus root and ginger. Add remaining oil and *miso*. Reduce flame to very low and cook for 3–4 hours. Stir frequently until liquid evaporates and mixture becomes as dry and black as possible.

Tekka helps to make the blood rich and strong and is high in protein, iron and Niacin. This is a very yang condiment, so use it very sparingly.

Garnishes

Garnishes are very important to use on soups, beans, salds, vegetable dishes, fish, etc. One reason is that they make the dish look very attractive to the eye. The other reason is that they stimulate the five different tastes such as sour, sweet, bitter, hot, pungent. It is very important to your health that these different tastes are stimulated. Often people only use one type of garnish which only stimulates one taste and the other four are left neglected. If this happens occasionally people become too yang or one-sided.

Some of the different types of garnishes that can be used are scallions, chives, parsley, celery leaves, watercress, *nori*, dulse, grated or shaved *daikon*, lemon, ginger, horseradish, *wasabi* (Japanese green horseradish), sesame seeds, *shiitake*, *kombu* strips, bonito flakes, dried fish, occasional orange slices or grapefruit slices, fruit slices, nuts, fresh mushrooms, sprig of fresh dill, etc.

When you place a bowl of rice on the table it is very attractive if you place a couple of sprigs of parsley or watercress in the center, for example.

Pickles

Pickles are a naturally fermented food. They aid in digestion, taste delicious, and are an important part of the macrobiotic way of eating. Pickling originated as a way to help people naturally adapt to the changing of the seasons. In temperate climates, pickling was developed as a way of naturally storing vegetables during the winter, while in hot climates, it was found that pickled vegetables did not easily spoil. Certain types of pickles also produce a naturally cooling effect during hot weather.

There are a wide variety of pickling methods. By varying such factors as time, pressure, salt and types of vegetables, you can produce either more yin or more yang pickles.

To maintain health, we should generally avoid the use of ingredients like spices, sugar, and vinegar when pickling. Macrobiotic pickles are usually made with salt, rice bran, wheat bran, *umeboshi*, rice flour, *tamari*, or *miso*.

Below are several basic methods for making your own pickles. If the pickles are too salty, simply soak them in cold water for about 1/2 hour before serving, to draw out the salt.

Salt Pickles

5 lbs. Chinese cabbage (2 large heads)
1/4–1/2 cup sea salt

A heavy ceramic or wooden crock or keg will be needed for this. Remove leaves from the cabbage and wash under cold water. Quarter and wash the cabbage hearts. Set both sections aside and let dry for about 24 hours. Place a thin layer of salt on the bottom of the crock, then a layer of cabbage leaves and hearts, and then another layer of salt. Repeat this until the cabbage is used or until the crock is filled. Place a lid or plate that will fit inside the crock on top of the cabbage and salt. Place a heavy rock or brick on top of the lid or plate. Cover with a thin layer of cheesecloth to keep the dust out. Store in a dark, cool place for 1–2 weeks or longer. Remove a portion, wash under cold water, slice and serve.

You may also pickle *daikon, daikon* leaves, carrots or other vegetables in this manner.

Rock or bricks

Plate or lid

Miso Pickles

Miso pickles are very yang and salty, and require no pressure. First brush the dirt from such root vegetables as *daikon* or carrots. Then tie a rope around them and hang in a shaded, warm spot for about 24 hours or until you can bend them in a semi-circle, to let the water evaporate. Place whole vegetables in the *miso* and leave for 1–2 years.

For a quicker *miso* pickle, cut the vegetables into rounds after drying and place in the *miso*. Leave for about 3–4 months.

Another variation is to cut the vegetables into thin slices and leave for 3 days to 1 week. To pickle a whole vegetable, cut small slits along its skin and leave in the *miso* for 1–2 weeks.

Tamari Pickles

Mix equal parts water and tamari in a bowl or glass jar. Slice vegetables such as rutabaga or turnips and place in *tamari*-water. Soak for 4 hours to 2 weeks, depending on the strength of pickle you desire.

Mustard Green Pickles

> 1 bunch mustard greens
> 1/2 cup tamari (or 1/4 cup water with 1/4 cup tamari)
> 2 tsp. ame (or yinnie syrup)
> 2 Tbsp. roasted sesame seeds
> 1 Tbsp. fresh grated ginger

Wash greens and cut into 1-inch lengths. Place greens in a quart jar, packing them firmly. Mix *tamari* and *ame* and place in pan. Bring to a boil and simmer until *ame* dissolves. Roast sesame seeds in a dry skillet and place in jar. Add grated ginger and *tamari* mixture to jar. Cover and refrigerate for 1 day. They are now ready to serve.

These pickles will keep for 1 week refrigerated.

For a variation, you may use turnip or *daikon* greens.

Rice Bran Pickles No. 1

Long Method (Ready in 3–5 Months)
> 10–12 cups nuka (rice bran)
> 1-1/2 to 2 cups sea salt
> 3–5 cups water

Short Method (Ready in 1–2 Weeks)
> 10–12 cups nuka
> 1/8–1/4 cup sea salt
> 3–5 cups water

Roast *nuka* (which is available in many natural food stores) in a dry skillet until it releases a nutty aroma. Allow to cool. Add salt to water and boil until the salt dissolves. Allow to cool. Mix water and salt with *nuka* to form a thick paste. Place paste in a wooden keg or ceramic crock and press down firmly.

When using root vegetables such as *daikon*, brush off soil and hang to dry in a shaded, warm place until you can bend them in a semi-circle.

Insert vegetables into the paste so that they are completely covered. Press the paste down until firm again. Keep in a cool room and cover with a thin piece of cheesecloth to keep the dust out and yet still allow the air to circulate. If water rises to the surface, add a little more roasted *nuka*.

Whole vegetables such as *daikon* may take from 3 to 5 months to pickle. More yin vegetables, such as Chinese cabbage, require only a week or two in the *nuka* paste. If you want a quicker pickle, simply slice vegetables very thin, tie in a cheesecloth sack and insert in the *nuka*. These take only a couple of days. Dried vegetables cut into rounds or 2- to 3-inch pieces, will also require less pickling time.

Whenever you add new vegetables, add a little more salt to the roasted *nuka* paste. In this way you can keep using the same paste for years. The amount of salt varies, depending on the size of the vegetable, type of vegetable, how long you leave it in the crock, and how full you fill the crock.

To serve, rinse vegetables under cold water to remove bran, and slice.

Rice Bran Pickles No. 2

Long Term (Ready in 3–5 Months)
　　10–12 cups of nuka (rice bran) or wheat bran
　　1-1/2 to 2 cups sea salt

Short Term (Ready in 1–2 Weeks)
　　10–12 cups nuka
　　1/8–1/4 cup sea salt

Combine *nuka* or wheat bran with salt and mix well. Place a layer of bran mixture on the bottom of a wooden keg or ceramic crock. Then place a layer of vegetables. Then sprinkle a layer of *nuka* on top of the vegetables. Repeat this layering until the *nuka* mixture is used up or until the crock is full. Always make sure that the *nuka* mixture is the top layer. Place a wooden disc or a plate inside the crock, on top of the vegetables and *nuka*. (The plate must be slightly smaller in circumference than the crock, so that it will fit inside.) Place a heavy weight, such as a rock or brick, on top of the plate. Soon water will begin to be squeezed out of the vegetables and rise to the surface of the crock. When this happens, replace the heavy weight on top of the plate with a lighter one. Cover with a thin layer of cheesecloth and store in a cool room.

To serve, rinse under cold water to remove bran and excess salt, and slice.

Cucumber Pickles

　　2–3 lbs. cucumbers
　　10–12 cups of water
　　1/4–1/3 cup sea salt
　　1 large onion halved then quartered
　　1–2 sprigs of fresh or dry dill

Combine water and salt. Bring to a boil and simmer 2–3 minutes until the salt dissolves. Allow to cool. Place washed cucumbers, dill, and onion slices in a large glass jar or a ceramic crock. Pour cooled salt water over the vegetables. Allow to sit uncovered in a dark, cool place for 3–4 days. Cover and refrigerate after 3–4 days. Cucumbers will keep for about one month in the refrigerator.

You may also pickle vegetables such as cauliflower, broccoli, carrots, or even watermelon rinds in the same manner.

Sauerkraut

5 lbs. cabbage (white kraut cabbage is best)
1/4–1/3 cup sea salt

Wash cabbage and slice very thin. Place cabbage in a wooden keg or ceramic crock. Sprinkle salt on cabbage and mix. Place a plate or wooden disc that is slightly smaller than the crock, on top of the cabbage, so that it fits down inside the crock. Place a heavy weight on top of the plate. Cover the top of the crock with a piece of cheesecloth. After one day, the water should cover the cabbage; if not, apply a heavier weight. Keep in a dark, cool place for 2 weeks. Check the crock daily. If mold forms on top, skim and discard. This mold is produced in the fermentation process and is not harmful, though it will give a moldy flavor to the sauerkraut if not removed.

To serve, rinse under cold water and place in a serving dish.

Daikon-Sauerkraut Pickles

This is a very light pickle that is not salty and is especially delicious and refreshing in the hot summer months.

1/2 gallon sauerkraut water
1 cup sauerkraut
2 large daikon sliced into rounds 1/4 inch thick

Slice *daikon* into rounds. Place in a glass jar. Cover with sauerkraut and sauerkraut water. Store uncovered jar in a cool place. After 3 days the pickles will be ready to eat.

To store, cover and refrigerate. They will keep for about one month.

You may re-use the water several times to make pickles, as long as it is kept refrigerated when not in use. Just add a little fresh sauerkraut and sauerkraut water before each use.

Umeboshi Pickles

7–8 umeboshi plums
daikon sliced into 1/4 inch rounds, or small whole red radishes, or sliced turnips

Place *umeboshi* in a large jar and add 2 quarts of water. Shake and let sit for a couple of hours so that the salt from the *umeboshi* dissolves into the water and the water turns pink. Place sliced vegetables or whole radishes into the water. Place uncovered jar in a cool place for 3 days. To store, cover and refrigerate.

Kyoto Style Pickles

Chinese Cabbage Pickles

**Chinese cabbage
sea salt
nuka (rice bran)**

Wash the cabbage and cut into quarters. Dry in the sum for two days. This will make the cabbage become very sweet. Sprinkle the bottom of the pickling crock with a small smount of sea salt. Put the dried cabbage into the crock, little by little, in layers. After each layer of cabbage, sprinkle with a small amount of sea salt. Repeat this until the crock is full or all of the cabbage is used. Place a lid, small enough to fit inside the crock, on top of the cabbage. The lid may be wood or ceramic. Then place a heavy stone on top of the lid.

When water from the cabbage rises up to the level of the stone, drain all the water out of the crock. Remove the cabbage from the crock.

Once again layer the cabbage. This time sprinkle *nuka* between each layer of cabbage. Replace the lid and stone on top of the cabbage. Keep in a cool place for about one week. The pickles are then ready to eat. Wash pickles under cold water, to remove bran, before slicing to serve.

The reason for draining the water off the pickles is because they are less salty tasting then and the cabbage taste more sweet. We must wait about one week for the *nuka* to produce enzymes. The smell will change during this one week period. Therefore the timing is determined by smell.

Turnip Pickles

**Turnips
Sea salt
Kombu**

Wash the turnips and cut in half. Then cut each half into thin slices. Sprinkle the bottom of the pickling crock with a small amount of sea salt. Place the turnips in the bowl, little by little, in layers. After each layer sprinkle with sea salt. Repeat until the crock is filled or until the turnips are used up.

Place a lid, small enough to fit inside the bowl, on top of the turnips. The lid may be wood or ceramic. Then place a stone on top of the lid.

When the water from the turnips rises up to the level of the stone, drain all of the water off. Remove the turnips from the bowl.

Cut the *kombu* into matchstick-sized pieces. Mix the turnips and *kombu*. Place turnips and *kombu* in the crock. Replace the lid and stone on top of the turnips. Keep in a cool place for one or two days. The turnips are now ready to eat.

The *kombu* will cause the water to thicken. The liquid should be very slippery, when you try to pick up the pickles. Refrigerate to store.

Bread

When making bread macrobiotically we usually avoid using yeast. Instead we rely upon the natural process of fermentation of grains or starters to raise the dough. Yeasted bread tends to bloat the stomach, weaken the intestines, thin the blood and I have noticed that it causes congestion in the sinuses, especially when used in combination with raisins and cinnamon. Yeasted bread should be eaten only occasionally, when dining at a restaurant, for instance, that does not have an unyeasted variety.

There are many different ways to make starters for producing breads that rise naturally. In a moment, I will briefly explain how to make one type.

It is not always necessary, however, to add a starter to bread to help it rise. If you let your bread dough sit in a warm place, covered with a damp towel, for 8 to 12 hours, it will naturally rise. There are many different kinds of bread which can be made simply by combining different flours, whole grains or fruit.

Kneading is the key in making unyeasted bread. The bread should be kneaded at least 350 times. The more you knead the better the chances of your bread rising.

If your bread does not turn out the first time you try, be patient. There have been many occasions when my bread would not rise. Besides kneading, there are a number of factors that influence making a good bread, including your mental and physical condition, the weather, the phase of the moon, how long you allow the dough to sit, etc. I have noticed that bread made during the full moon rises better than at other times. On the other hand, bread made on a rainy day does not rise as much as on a sunny day. I have also noticed that if I am in a happy, peaceful, positive mood my bread is much better. Occasionally my 3-1/2 year old son helps me make bread, a task he greatly enjoys. He is happy to help and really puts a great deal of enthusiasm and happiness into the kneading. The bread has never failed to turn out well whenever he lends a hand.

Bread containing some type of whole grain such as rice, sweet rice, barley, or millet, is much easier to digest than bread made solely from flour. Whole grain bread is actually a meal in itself.

In my bread recipes I have used oil, but it is not a necessary ingredient. In many European countries oil is not used. In this case, the bread will come out a little heavier but still very delicious. In any of the recipes below the choice of using oil is yours.

Rice Bread

    4 cups whole wheat flour
    4 cups cooked brown rice
    2 Tbsp. sesame oil (optional)
    1/4–1/2 tsp. sea salt
    water

Mix flour and sea salt. Add oil and mix. Add rice and sift the mixture through your hands until the rice is completely mixed in. Add enough water to form the dough into a ball. Knead from 300 to 350 times (approximately 10–15 minutes). While kneading, the dough occasionally becomes moist and sticky. When this happens, sprinkle a small amount of flour on the dough and continue kneading. This may happen 4 or 5 times during the kneading process.

Oil two bread pans with sesame oil. Place dough in pans and pat down. Press the dough down all along the edges of the pan to create a rounded effect and then make a small slit in its center. Put a damp towel over the pans and let sit for 8–12 hours in a warm place. Bake at 300 degrees for 15–20 minutes, then at 350 degrees F. for 1 hour and 15 minutes.

If the rice is two or three days old, the bread will be much sweeter. Also, slightly sour rice will help the bread rise better and will produce a sweet taste.

Raisin-Rice Bread

   4 cups cooked brown rice
   4 cups whole wheat flour
   2 cups raisins
   1/4–1/2 tsp. sea salt
   2 Tbsp. sesame oil (optional)
   water

Prepare same way as rice bread. After you have kneaded the bread about 250 times, add the raisins and knead 50–100 times more. Place in oiled bread pans and cover with a damp towel. Set in a warm place for 8–12 hours. Bake same as for rice bread.

Amasake Bread

   4 cups whole wheat flour
   4 cups amasake
   1/4–1/2 tsp. sea salt
   2 Tbsp. sesame oil (optional)
   water

This bread can be made in the same way as plain rice bread. (See Dessert section for *amasake* recipe.) It has a very sweet taste. Also, since the *amasake* is fermented, it gives the bread a slightly yeasted taste without the yinnizing, or expansive, effects of regular yeast.

Wholewheat Bread

   8 cups whole wheat flour
   2 Tbsp. sesame oil (optional)
   1/4–1/2 tsp. sea salt
   water

Mix flour and sea salt. Add oil, and mix thoroughly with flour by sifting through hands. Add enough water to form a ball of dough. Knead about 300–350 times. Oil two bread pans with sesame oil. Place dough in pans. Cover with a damp towel and let sit for 8–12 hours in a warm place to rise. Bake at 300 degrees F. for 15 minutes, then at 350 degrees F. for 1 hour 15 minutes longer.

Sourdough Starter

A sourdough starter can be made by mixing one cup of flour and enough water to make a thick batter. Cover the bowl with a damp towel and set it in a warm place for 3–4 days. As it ferments, it will start to bubble and turn sour. This starter may be added to any of the whole grain bread recipes to make bread rise. Simply add 1 to 1-1/2 cups of the starter to your bread dough and knead as explained above. Cover with a damp towel and set in a warm place for 8–12 hours. Then bake in the same manner as rice bread. Your bread will have a slightly sour, delicious taste.

Such items as sour whole grain, sour noodle water, or sour starch water (which results from making *seitan* and letting the starch water sit in a warm place for 3–4 days) can be used as a starter for bread. These starters can also be used in making cakes, waffles, pancakes, and muffins.

Corn Bread

> **3 cups corn meal**
> **1 cup pastry flour**
> **1/4 tsp. sea salt**
> **2 Tbsp. corn oil (optional)**
> **2–3 cups cold water**

Mix flour and salt. Add oil and mix thoroughly. Add water and stir. Pre-heat oven to 375 degrees F. Oil bread or cake pan with sesame oil and place the empty oiled pan in the oven for 5 minutes to heat the oil. Remove the pan and place the corn bread mixture in it. If your bread is made with 2 cups of water, bake at 375 degrees F. for 1 hour 15 minutes. If 3 cups of water were used in the mixture, bake for 1 hour 45 minutes, at the same temperature.

I usually add 3 cups of water, as it makes the bread softer and sweeter. As a variation, add 1 cup of cooked brown rice to the batter or 1 cup of cooked millet. The rice will make the bread very light, sweet and delicious. The millet will make the bread somewhat dryer, but also sweet and delicious.

Steamed Bread

Last year Mrs. Kushi received 40 loaves of bread from the East West Foundation after a residential program. She distributed them around to the different study houses. It was very hard and dried-out. She steamed the bread, and it tasted like it had been freshly baked. If you have bread that is old and dried-out, you can slice or leave whole. Steam the slices for 2–4 minutes or longer for a whole loaf. This brings new life to the bread and is very moist and delicious. I have noticed that when the bread is steamed that it reduces my desire for using nut butters on bread as it is very moist.

Desserts including *Amasake*

I have found that the best desserts are made by using natural sweeteners such as seasonal fruits, raisins, dried fruit, apple juice, barley malt or rice syrup (yinnie syrup), rather than honey or maple syrup.

Barley malt is made from barley which has been soaked, sprouted, and cooked. Rice syrup, or *ame*, is made in the same way, from whole rice and barley. *Ame* can also be made from wheat.

I have found that it is best to avoid the use of spices in dessert cooking whenever possible. I have included two pie recipes which use cinnamon. Cinnamon comes from the bark of a tropical evergreen tree which grows in Indonesia, China, and Southeast Asia. It seems to be the least yin of the tropical spices, but it still should be used sparingly and only occasionally. The recipes calling for cinnamon will turn out delicious if this optional ingredient is omitted.

Fresh grated ginger root may also be used occasionally as a spice. I have found that all other spices are extremely yin and are especially bad for the heart, circulation, and sinus. In macrobiotic baking we avoid using eggs and milk. Macrobiotic desserts may not be as light and airy as those which you are used to, but you will notice that they are more wholesome.

Be careful about your use of oil when baking. It is possible to make a very delicious, light pastry, without using large amounts of oil. In baking, I use either sesame or corn oil, depending on the results desired. Sesame oil has a stronger taste, while corn oil makes a pastry lighter, and crispier.

Basic Dough (2 crusts)

4 cups wholewheat pastry flour
1/4 tsp. sea salt
1/8–1/4 cup corn oil
3/4–1 cup cold water

Mix flour and salt. Add oil and sift through your hands, using a rubbing motion so as to evenly coat the flour with the oil. Add water gradually to form a dough. The dough should not be sticky. If it is, add a bit more flour. Knead into a ball. Do not knead very long, since the oil may start to be absorbed through your skin. Let sit for a few minutes. Sprinkle flour on a board and rolling pin. Roll out dough. You can easily place the dough in a pie plate by rolling it up on the rolling pin and then placing it in a pie plate. Use about half of the dough for the bottom crust and add desired filling. Then, roll out the remaining half. Wet the edge of the bottom crust with a small amount of water to help seal the pie crusts, and place the remaining pie crust on top of the filled pie plate. To seal the crusts, wet a fork and press around the edges, or you may pinch it together with your thumbs. Make four small slits in the top center of the pie crust so it will not crack when baking.

For a pie with only a bottom crust, partially prebake the crust in a pie plate for about 10 minutes at 375 degrees F. Make two or three small slits in the bottom of the crust before baking to avoid bubbling. Then, fill the baked crust and bake again until done (approximately 30 minutes).

Apple Pie No. 1

10–12 medium apples sliced (remove skin if non-organic)
pinch of sea salt
1/4–1/2 cup rice syrup (yinnie syrup or ame)
1–2 Tbsp. arrowroot
1/4–1/2 tsp. cinnamon (optional)

Use above method for pie crust. Place bottom crust in pie plate. Mix all above ingredients together and fill pie shell. Add top crust and seal. Cut four small slits in top and bake at 375 degrees F. for approximately 30–35 minutes or until crust turns golden brown. To test whether apples are done, insert a chopstick into one of the slits in the crust.

Apple Pie No. 2

   10–12 medium apples sliced
   pinch of sea salt
   1/4–1/2 cup raisins
   1–2 Tbsp. arrowroot

Mix above ingredients. Place crust in pie plate and fill bottom crust. Place top crust on filling. Seal edges and trim excess dough. Make four slits in top crust. Bake at 375 degrees F. for 30–35 minutes, or until golden brown.

Apple/Squash Pie

   1 medium buttercup squash cubed
   4–5 medium apples sliced
   pinch of sea salt

Place squash and apples in a pot with just enough water to lightly cover the bottom of the pot. Cover, and cook until squash becomes soft. Purée in a Foley food mill. Place filling in partially baked pie shell. Bake at 375 degrees F. for 25–30 minutes or until crust is golden brown. You may also place sliced apples or sprinkle chopped walnuts around the edge of the pie filling before baking to make a more attractive and delicious dish.

Unsweetened Squash Pie with Oatmeal Crust

   1 large buttercup squash or Hokkaido pumpkin peeled and cubed
   1 medium onion diced
   pinch of sea salt
   1/4–1/2 cup water

Place cubed squash and diced onions in a pot. Add salt and water. Cook until squash is soft, and purée in a Foley food mill. Then, evenly distribute puréed squash and onions in a partially baked oatmeal crust. Bake at 375 degrees F. for approximately 25–30 minutes, or until crust is golden brown.

Oatmeal Crust

   3 cups rolled oats
   1-1/2 cups whole wheat pastry flour
   2–3 Tbsp. corn oil
   1/4 tsp. sea salt
   2 cups water

Mix oats, salt, and flour. Add oil and mix again. Add water to form thick batter. Spread batter evenly on an oiled cookie sheet and bake at 375 degrees F. for approximately 10 minutes. Remove from oven and place desired filling evenly on crust and bake again at 375 degrees F. for 25–30 minutes.

Squash Pie

1 large buttercup squash or Hokkaido pumpkin peeled and cubed
1 cup rice syrup (yinnie syrup or ame)
1/4 tsp. sea salt
1/4 tsp. cinnamon (optional)
1/2 cup chopped walnuts
1/4 cup water

Cook squash in pot with approximately 1/4 cup water and salt. Cook until squash is soft. Purée in a Foley food mill. This purée should be thick. If it is too thick, add a little water. If too thin, cook on a low flame until water evaporates. Then, add yinnie syrup, and, if desired, cinnamon.

Place crust in pie plate and cut two or three small slits in bottom. Partially bake at 375 degrees F. for 10 minutes. Remove from oven and fill with purée. Sprinkle finely chopped walnuts around the edge of the fillings and bake at 375 degrees F. for 30 minutes, or until the crust is golden brown.

Oatmeal Raisin Cookies (24 cookies)

3 cups rolled oats
1-1/2 cups whole wheat pastry flour
3 Tbsp. corn oil
1/4 tsp. sea salt
1 cup raisins
2 cups cold water

Mix rolled oats, flour, and salt with spoon. Add oil and mix again. Add water to make thick batter. Add raisins. (You may add 1/2 cup chopped walnuts for a different flavor. If you add walnuts you may need to add just slightly more water to batter.) Spoon batter onto oiled cookie sheet and pat down to form cookie. Do not make them too thick or they will take longer to bake and they will not cook properly. They should be crisp. Each cookie should be about two inches in diameter and about 1/4–1/3 inch thick. Bake at 375 degrees F. for 25–30 minutes or until golden brown.

Kanten

Kanten is a very light, refreshing dessert made from a type of seaweed called agar-agar. You may use almost any kind of seasonal fruit in making *kanten*, such as strawberries, blueberries, peaches, pears, nectarines, raspberries, melon, apples, raisins, and others. You can also use the agar-agar flakes, along with vegetables and vegetable soup stock to make an aspic instead of a dessert. *Azuki* beans and raisins are also very delicious when jelled with the agar-agar flakes.

Prepackaged agar-agar flakes are available in most natural food stores. Some packages have different directions printed on them than those used below, so consult those directions before making *kanten*.

> **3 medium apples sliced**
> **1 quart water or you may use a 1/2 water, 1/2 apple juice combination**
> **pinch of sea salt**
> **6 Tbsp. agar-agar flakes or one bar (read directions)**

Bring liquid, salt, and agar-agar flakes to a boil. Reduce flame to low and simmer about 15 minutes. Add sliced apples the last 5 minutes. Stir occasionally. Pour into a dish or mold and refrigerate until jelled (about 45 minutes to 1 hour).

When using other fruits, cook same as above, with the exception of melon. Do not cook the melon, but simply place it in a bowl and pour the hot liquid over the pieces. If you decide to use plain water in your *kanten*, you may add 1/2 cup of raisins to sweeten. Just add the raisins at the same time you add the apples and cook as above.

When making a vegetable aspic, use very thin sliced or shaved vegetables and 1 quart of vegetable stock and cook the vegetables approximately 5–10 minutes after you add them to the flakes and vegetable stock.

When making an *azuki* bean-raisin aspic, cook the *azuki* beans and raisins until the beans are done (approximately 1-1/2 hours). Then add to 1 quart of water, sea salt, and flakes and cook as above.

Agar-agar is very good for constipation due to an over-yang condition.

Apple Crisp (Pear Crisp or Peach Crisp)

Crust:
> **1 cup rolled oats**
> **1/2 cup chopped walnuts**
> **1/4 cup chopped or slivered almonds**
> **1/4 cup chopped filberts**
> **2 Tbsp. rice syrup (yinnie syrup or ame)**

Filling:
> **10–12 sliced apples, pears, or peaches (leave skin on if organic)**
> **pinch of sea salt**
> **2 Tbsp. arrowroot**
> **1/4–1/2 cup water**

Slice apples, pears or peaches. Add salt and arrowroot. Mix together and place in a baking dish.

In a dry skillet roast oats until golden brown on a medium-low flame. Place in a bowl. Roast nuts in a dry skillet on a medium-low flame until they release a fragrant aroma. Remove and chop. Add nuts to rolled oats and mix. Add yinnie syrup and mix with your hands to coat oat and nut mixture with yinnie.

Sprinkle oat/nut mixture evenly over apples, pears or peaches. Add water, cover and bake at 375 degrees F. for 20–25 minutes. Remove cover and bake 5–10 minutes more to brown oat/nut topping.

Apple Sauce

Wash and peel apples. Slice and place in a pot with a small amount of water (1/4–1/2 cup), just enough to keep the apples from burning, as they normally become very watery when cooked. Add pinch of sea salt, and simmer for 10 minutes or until soft. Purée in a Foley food mill and serve.

Baked Apples

Wash apples and bake at 375 degrees F. until done, approximately 20 minutes. You may, for variety, core the apples and fill with a mixture of *miso*, *tahini*, raisins or *miso* and *tahini*. For filling use 6 tablespoons of *tahini*, 2 teaspoons of brown rice *miso*, and 1/4 cup raisins. Mix together and spoon into cored apple.

Raisin Strudel

   2 cups raisins
   1 cup chopped walnuts
   pinch of sea salt
   1/2 cup water

Place raisins, water, and salt in a sauce pan and bring to a boil. Simmer until liquid is cooked away. Allow to cool. Mix raisins with the walnuts.

Make a pastry dough and roll out as you would for a pie crust, only thinner. Spread filling evenly on the crust and roll it up in a log shape. Seal both ends of the strudel to prevent the juice from spilling out. This is done by folding up the ends slightly and pressing down. Place on an oiled cookie sheet and bake at 375 degrees F. for approximately 30 minutes or until the crust is golden brown. Remove from oven and slice the strudel into 1/2–1 inch rounds.

A strudel can be made with almost any seasonal fruit and nuts.

You can make a simple, yet delicious strudel filling by spreading a small amount of barley malt or yinnie syrup evenly on a rolled crust. (If you wet your hands slightly it is easier to spread.) Then sprinkle a small amount of cinnamon (1/4 tsp. per crust) on the yinnie syrup and spread evenly with your fingers.

Sprinkle chopped walnuts on top of the yinnie. Roll up strudel and bake same as above recipe.

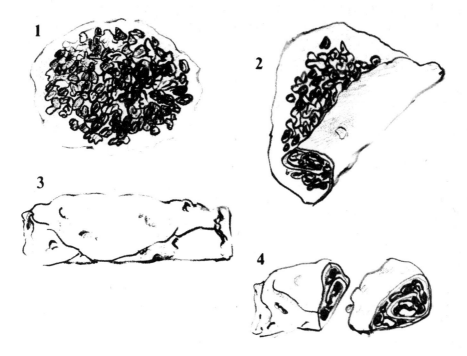

Berry Pies

Cook berries with small amount of water and sweeten, if necessary, with yinnie syrup. Add pinch of sea salt and thicken with diluted *kuzu* or arrowroot flour to desired thickness. Fill partially baked pie shell with berry mixture. Bake at 375 degrees F. until crust is golden brown (approximately 25–30 minutes).

Sweet Azuki Beans

Cook 2 cups *azuki* beans for about 20 minutes. Add 1-1/2 cups raisins. Cook until 80% done. Then add 1/2 teaspoon of sea salt and either 1 cup of dried apples or 3 sliced fresh apples. Cook until beans are done. When beans are done turn up flame and boil off excess water.

You may eat as is or you can oil a baking dish and place a layer of approximately 4 cups of *mochi* (cooked sweet rice as explained in the section on Grains) on the bottom of the dish and spread a layer of sweet *azuki* beans on top. Bake at 375 degrees F. for 10 minutes, which is just enough time to heat up the *mochi* and *azuki* beans. Do not bake longer as the *mochi* will expand and spill over onto your oven. Serve hot or cool.

Apple Tart

8 medium apples sliced
1/2 cup raisins
1/4 cup chopped walnuts
pinch of sea salt
1–2 Tbsp. arrowroot

Mix all ingredients. Roll out pie crust and place on an oiled cookie sheet. Place apple mixture on one half of the crust, and fold the other half over to cover the apples. Turn the edges of the crust up and pinch together to seal. Bake at 375 degrees F. for 30–40 minutes, or until golden brown. Slice are serve.

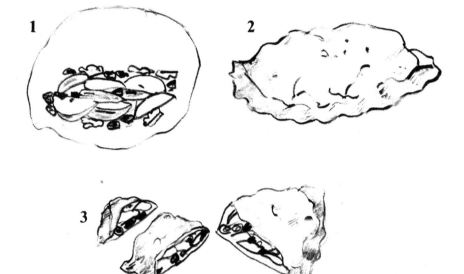

Amasake

Amasake is a natural sweetener made from fermented sweet rice. It can be used as a sweetener for cookies and cakes, pancakes and donuts, and in making bread. *Amasake* can also be blended in a food mill, placed in a sauce pan with a pinch of sea salt and a little boiling water, brought to a boil and then served hot or cool as a drink.

4 cups sweet brown rice
1/2 cups koji (special bacteria needed to begin fermentation)
8 cups water

Wash rice, drain and soak overnight in 8 cups of water. Place rice in a pressure-cooker. Bring to pressure. Reduce flame and cook for 20 minutes. Turn off flame and let the rice sit in pressure-cooker for 45 minutes. When the rice is cool enough to handle with your hands, mix in the *koji* and allow the mixture to ferment at least 4 hours but no longer than 8 hours. Do this by placing the rice and *koji* in a glass bowl. (Do not use a metal mixing bowl.) Cover the bowl with a towel and keep the rice warm during the process of fermentation. This can be done by placing the bowl in an oven with just the pilot light on or keeping it near a radiator. Several times during the period of fermentation mix the ingredients so that the *koji* will melt. Place rice in a pot, bring to a boil. As soon as it starts to bubble, turn the flame off. Allow to cool. Place rice in a glass bowl or jar and refrigerate.

To keep for a long time, *amasake* should be cooked over a low flame until it becomes a brown color.

When using as a sweetener, you may either add as is to pastries or blend first to make it smooth.

Fish

Among the many varieties of fish and shellfish, the red, or darkmeat fish are the most yang. These include tuna, red snapper, herring, sardines, and salmon. White-meat fish such as sole, flounder, and haddock are generally more yin. Among shellfish, oysters, clams, mussels and octopus are more yin, while shrimp, crab and lobster are more yang. It is generally preferable to eat the more yin varieties of fish and shellfish.

Sashimi

Sashimi is the Japanese name for fish that is cut into thin strips and served raw. It usually comes with a dip sauce made with *tamari*, water, and grated ginger, *daikon*, or horseradish. The preparation of *sashimi* requires skill with a very sharp knife and a knowledge of how to properly bone and slice a fish. However, you can begin preparing *sashimi* by using an already boned fillet of red snapper, striped bass, tuna, sole, or other type of fish. Slice the fish into diagonal strips, using a very sharp knife. The strips should be no more than 1/4 inch thick. To serve, simply arrange the slices on a platter along with boiled, steamed, or raw vegetables, and grated *daikon*. Your *sashimi* should be beautifully arranged as well as delicious. Raw fish, though still having animal food qualities, can be more yin than some root vegetables. For this reason, *sashimi* is an excellent way to take fish.

Baked Fish

Quickly wash fish, and cover with a mixture containing an equal amount of *tamari* and water, and a small amount of grated ginger. Allow the fish to marinate in the mixture for about 1 hour. Then, place fish in a lightly oiled baking dish, cover and bake at 375 degrees F. until almost done. Remove cover, and finish baking the fish. The total baking time should be approximately 15–20 minutes, depending on the size, thickness, and type of fish, as well as the type of baking dish that you are using.

Another way of baking fish is to simply place washed fish on a baking dish or cookie sheet and squeeze a little lemon juice and *tamari* over it. Bake as above.

When you remove the fish from the baking dish, arrange it on a platter with slices of lemon and parsley sprigs, or with grated *daikon*.

Stuffed Shrimp

   3 cups dry roasted whole wheat bread crumbs
   1 medium onion diced
   1 stalk diced celery with leaves
   10 jumbo shrimp
   1/2 cup water
   1 tsp. tamari
   1 Tbsp. corn oil

Cut bread into 1/4 or 1/2 inch cubes and roast in a dry skillet until golden brown and slightly crunchy. Lightly brush another skillet with 1 tablespoon of corn oil and sauté onions and celery until onions are transparent. Mix with bread crumbs. Add 1/2 cup water and 1 teaspoon of *tamari*. Wash shrimp and remove blue vein from center by making a small slice down the underside. Place shrimp on bottom of baking dish. Spread the bread crumb mixture evenly over the shrimp. Cover the dish and bake at 375 degrees F. until almost done (approximately 15–20 minutes). Do not over-cook or the shrimp will become tough. Remove cover and bake for another 5 minutes to brown the stuffing and evaporate any remaining liquid.

You can also prepare stuffed flounder, scrod, or other fish in the same manner.

Broiled Fish

Marinate fish in the same manner as for baking and place on a baking sheet under the broiler. Broil until done. This should take about 5 minutes, depending on the size, type, and thickness of the fish.

Instead of marinating the fish, you can squeeze lemon juice and a few drops of *tamari* on it. Broil as above.

Arrange fish on a platter with slices of carrot, cucumber, parsley, or watercress, along with a little grated *daikon*.

Pan-Fried Fish

Marinate fish for 30 minutes to an hour in a mixture of equal parts *tamari* and water and a small amount of grated ginger. Dry with a towel, and roll in corn or pastry floor. Place in a skillet with 1/8–1/4 inch oil and fry until golden brown on one side. Turn over and fry until golden brown on the other side.

You may also simply fry the fish in a very small amount of oil without rolling it in flour.

Tempura

Cut fish fillets into 2 or 3 inch pieces. If you are using shellfish, remove shells and veins and *tempura* whole. When preparing shrimp *tempura*, make two small diagonal slits in the underside of the shrimp to prevent it from curling up. Roll fish or shellfish in whole wheat or whole wheat pastry flour, and dip into *tempura* batter (see section on Vegetable *Tempura* for batter recipe.) *Tempura* until golden brown on one side. Turn over and brown other side. This takes only a few minutes. Drain fish on a paper towel.

Fish Soup Stock or Sauce

Boil fish bones, head, or leftovers for several minutes in a pot of water. Remove by straining through cheesecloth, or you may tie the various parts in a cheesecloth sack and boil the entire sack. Use the water as a stock or thicken with pastry flour to make a fish sauce and season with *tamari*.

There are many other dishes that can be made with fish such as baked stuffed clams, fish patties, croquettes, dumplings, salads, etc. Please experiment.

Leftovers

In most cooking classes I am asked what to do with leftovers. One of the most basic principles of macrobiotics is that we should waste as little as possible, so never throw anything away that is in any way edible. There are practically unlimited ways to use leftovers to create entirely new, attractive and delicious dishes.

An entire cookbook could be devoted to preparing leftovers. I would like to briefly explain a few suggestions which may help you make new dishes from leftover food.

At first it may seem difficult to prepare a meal from leftovers. Try to use your imagination.

Grains

Brown Rice

If you have leftover rice, you may add chopped or sliced vegetables and fry the rice. Leftover *azuki* bean rice is delicious when fried with a few scallions. You may use rice in making rice bread or add it to corn bread. Rice added to corn bread makes the bread very sweet and easy to digest. You may also use leftover rice in stuffed cabbage. Adding diced onions, carrots, or other combinations of vegetables to the rice, roll it up in partially boiled cabbage leaves and cook as you would stuffed cabbage and *seitan*.

You may also make rice balls with leftover rice. If you have old rice balls, or *sushi* that have become dry and hard, you can deep-fry them for a tasty treat. Also, if you add diced vegetables like onions, carrots, and celery along with a little pastry flour to your leftover rice, you can mold it into small croquettes and *tempura*. When you have browned or burnt rice on the bottom of your pressure-cooker, place it on a plate or straw mat to dry. When it becomes hard and dry, you can deep fry it to make a delicious, crunchy snack.

You may also make a vegetable rice pie by mixing your leftover rice with vegetables and a little water, and baking the mixture in a pie crust in the same way as you would a fruit pie.

Leftover rice can also be mixed with *seitan* and vegetables and used to stuff a hubbard squash. This "squash turkey" is a favorite in our house around Thanksgiving and Christmas. You can also stuff buttercup squash or Hokkaido squash.

Leftover rice can also be used to make delicious soups such as those outlined under "grain soups." Leftover sweet rice makes a great soup when cooked with onions, carrots, and celery.

You can also make soft rice for breakfast by adding four or five cups of water to one cup of leftover rice and cooking it on a low flame in a pressure-cooker or a pot for 35–40 minutes.

These are just a few of the many ways you can use leftover brown rice.

Millet

Leftover millet can be used in making millet soup. Diced, leftover *seitan* is a wonderful compliment when added to it.

Millet added to corn bread is very delicious. You can also add diced onions, celery, and a little flour to your millet to make croquettes which can be baked, pan fried, or deep fried. Leftover millet can be used to make millet bread, or you can add 4 cups of water to one cup of millet to make a soft millet breakfast cereal.

Barley

Leftover barley can be used instead of rice, in the rice bread recipe. It can also be cooked with lentils, celery, onions and mushrooms to create a soup. Other beans can also be cooked with barley to make a delicious soup.

Buckwheat

If you have leftover buckwheat, you can make a delicious *Kasha Varnitchkes* by sautéing the buckwheat with a diced onion and cooked whole wheat elbow macaroni.

You can add chopped vegetables to your kasha and make stuffed cabbage, or you can make a pastry dough and wrap it around the kasha and vegetables to make *Kasha Knishes*, which you can then bake in the oven until the dough is golden brown.

You can also make a kasha soup by adding diced onions and celery, and season with *tamari*.

Baked kasha is especially good when served with a bechamel sauce. Add sliced cabbage, diced onions, sliced carrots, sliced mushrooms and a little water and *tamari* to kasha and bake it in the oven.

Whole or Rolled Oats

Mix equal portions of leftover oats and leftover rice and cook with four parts water to create a creamy breakfast cereal, or use leftover oats to make a creamy *miso* soup. You can also substitute oats for rice or in combination with rice to make whole grain bread.

Noodles

Leftover noodles can be fried with vegetables, or used in combination with other grains, beans or vegetables to prepare a soup.

To make a delicious noodle casserole, *tempura* vegetables such as onions, mushrooms and carrots, and layer the *tempuraed* vegetables and noodles in a baking dish. Add a little water and *tamari* and bake.

You can make a refreshing noodle salad by adding boiled or raw vegetables to cooked noodles and mixing with a small amount of *umeboshi* or *tahini* salad dressing.

Seitan

Leftover *seitan* can be cooked in soup with grain or noodles, or can be baked with beans. It can also be mixed with rice and vegetables and fried or used to stuff cabbage rolls. *Seitan* can be used in preparing salads, sandwiches, or vegetable dishes or can be combined with vegetables to make a *seitan*-vegetable pie. Sautéed *seitan*, kale, and carrots make a nice dish, while *seitan* boiled or sautéed with cabbage is also very delicious.

Seitan can be dipped in a batter and *tempuraed*, or added to a vegetable *sukiyaki*. If you have *tamari* water left over from cooking *seitan*, use it as a soup stock or, by adding *kuzu* and diced onions, you can create a delicious sauce. A different sauce can be made by adding celery and diced onions to the starch water left from rinsing the *seitan*. You can make an interesting chow mein sauce by adding mung bean sprouts, celery, snow peas, mushrooms and diced onions to *kuzu* or starch water sauce. Serve over noodles that have been boiled, drained, and then deep fried until golden brown.

Beans

There are numerous ways to use leftover beans. They can be added to soups, or combined with onions, carrots, or *seitan* to make a delicious baked dish. You can make a bean pie, or fry leftover beans with rice or whole wheat shells or elbow macaroni. Some beans, such as kidney, green or waxed beans, can be used in making a bean salad. *Azuki* beans can be cooked with raisins and agar-agar to make a bean aspic.

Vegetables

As long as your cooked vegetables have not soured, they can be used again in another dish. You can make a vegetable pie, or, if the vegetables are in large pieces, you can wrap them in pastry dough and bake until the crust is golden brown, slice and serve. Leftover vegetables can also be added to soups, bean, seaweed or noodle dishes. When using leftover vegetables in other dishes, add them toward the end of cooking so that they will not become mushy.

Leftover sweet corn can be removed from the cob and mixed with corn flour, pastry flour, diced onions, celery and a little water and either pan fried or deep fried to create corn fritters. If you don't have enough vegetables for a soup, simply boil them in water for several minutes and use the water as a soup stock. Save all your vegetable juices for soup stock or for use as a base for making a bechamel or *kuzu* sauce. Leftover vegetables can also be wrapped in *seitan* to make croquettes.

Soups

Leftover grain soups take on a new taste with the addition of a little *miso*. They are also good with leftover *seitan*. Soups such as lentil or kidney bean can be completely transformed by adding a few whole wheat elbow macaronis or shells, or use barley instead of noodles. Some soups can be changed into a new dish simply by adding a few vegetables. Grain soups also take on a new quality when a few beans are added.

Seaweed

If you have leftover *arame* or *hijiki*, prepare a pastry dough, rolling it out as you would for a pie crust. Spread the seaweed evenly on the crust, and roll it up as you would strudel. Bake at 375 degrees F. for approximately 30 minutes or until golden brown, slice and serve. You can also make individual tarts or a seaweed pie.

A leftover *wakame* and onions dish can also be added to *miso*, kidney bean, rice, barley, or millet soup.

Leftover *kombu* can be used several times for soup stock, or made into *kombu* soup by adding onions, carrots, water and *tamari*. You can also cut it into 1-inch pieces and either bake or simmer with carrots, onions and burdock, or with other vegetables. Leftover *kombu* can be used to make *Shio Kombu*.

Nori can be used as a garnish on soups and noodles, or is delicious when added to fried rice.

Bread

If you have old bread which is dried out or slightly molded, remove the mold, cube, deep fry, and use as a garnish for soups or as a stuffing for squash when combined with onions, celery and *seitan*. You can also steam old bread and it will regain its flavor and freshness.

Fish

Leftover fish can be used in fish soup, as well as in sauces or soup stock. To make fish croquettes, finely chop the leftover fish, mix with a little flour, diced onion, celery and *tamari*. These can be baked, pan fried or deep fried.

Beverages

The best beverages for our health are those that do not contain artificial dyes, preservatives, sugar, caffeine, or other artificial ingredients. Grain coffee, grain teas, and other high-quality, non-stimulant teas are suitable for regular use, while beer or *sake*, which are made from grains, can be used occasionally for enjoyment.

Bancha Tea

Bancha or *Kukicha* tea is probably the best tea for daily use. It contains 3 times as much calcium per 100 grams as does milk, and helps aid in digestion. *Bancha* tea is made from the twigs of the *bancha* tea bush.

Dry roast twigs in skillet for 2–3 minutes, while constantly stirring and shaking the pan so as to prevent the twigs from burning. Remove from skillet and store in air-tight jar. To prepare tea, add 2 tablespoons of roasted twigs to 1-1/2 quarts water and bring to a boil. Reduce flame and simmer for several minutes. For a lighter tea, add only 1 tablespoon of twigs to the same amount of water, bring to a boil, turn off flame, and let twigs steep in water. These twigs can be used several times. Simply add more water or twigs when necessary. Clean pot and replace twigs about once a week.

Grain Tea

Dry roast any grain over medium flame for about 10 minutes, stirring constantly and shaking pan occasionally. Brown rice and unhulled barley make an especially good tea. Add 2–3 tablespoons of roasted grain to 1-1/2 quarts of water. Bring to a boil, reduce flame, and simmer 10–15 minutes.

Mix roasted rice with *bancha* for a different flavor of tea.

Mugicha

Mugicha is made from unhulled, roasted barley, and can be found in most natural food stores. To prepare your own *mugicha*, roast unhulled barley in dry skillet until very dark brown. Cook as for other grain teas.

Umeboshi Tea

This tea has a cooling effect and helps to replace mineral salts which are lost through perspiration.

Remove meat from pits of 2–3 *umeobshi* plums and add to 1 quart of water. Bring to a boil, reduce flame, and simmer for about 1/2 hour.

Grain Coffee

There are many grain coffees available in natural food stores. Use one that does not have figs, dates, molasses, or honey added to it.

The best grain coffee I have found is called *Yannoh*, and is made from five different grains and beans. In Europe it is sold prepackaged. It is not available in America as yet, but is easily made by separately roasting 3 cups of brown rice, 2-1/2 cups of wheat, 1-1/2 cups of *azuki* beans, 2 cups of chickpeas and 1 cup chicory root. Roast ingredients until dark brown, then mix together and grind into a fine powder in a grain mill. Use 1 tablespoon of *yannoh* per cup of water. Bring to a boil, reduce flame, simmer for about 5–10 minutes, and serve.

Mu Tea

Mu tea is made from 16 different herbs. It is a more yang beverage, and is good for the stomach. It may be used in cold or hot weather. *Mu* tea is sold prepackaged in most natural food stores. Simmer 1 package in a quart of water for about 10 minutes. It is good as an occasional supplement to *bancha*.

Mugwort Tea

Mugwort is a more yin beverage that is used mostly for medicinal purposes rather than as a daily beverage. It can be used to treat overly-yang conditions such as jaundice, and has been found to be effective in helping to rid the body of worms. To prepare, add about 1 tablespoon dried mugwort to 2 cups of water and simmer approximately 5–10 minutes. Don't continue use for more than several days as too much of this tea can cause constipation.

Apple Juice or Cider

If your condition is generally good, you may enjoy an occasional glass of apple cider. In the summer, apple juice can be served cool or lightly chilled, but not icy cold, as this has a paralyzing effect on the digestive tract. In cool weather, heat the cider and drink hot. This can help neutralize an overly-yang condition resulting from the intake of too much salt. However, persons with overly-yin conditions should avoid apple juice until their condition improves.

Medicinal Cooking

The best way to cure sickness is through your daily food. In some cases, this approach may take more time than symptomatic treatments, but it is the only way to relieve the cause of sickness. Whenever an illness appears, reflect on those things you have done to produce it. Recall what you have eaten, or what you ate in the past that may now be discharging.

When people first begin eating macrobiotically, they may experience various types of adjustments due to their past eating habits. These may manifest as colds, fever, sore throats, aches and pains, headaches, diarrhea, constipation, or in other ways. Such discharges are nothing but the elimination of sugar, animal food, dairy, drugs, and other accumulations from the body. Since they are a sign that the body is ridding itself of past excess, they are actually beneficial and serve to keep our condition clean.

I would now like to offer several simply prepared home remedies that will help to relieve any discomfort experienced by these adjustments, and to help you to discharge past foods more comfortably and smoothly.

Ginger Compress (Fomentation)

Ginger compresses are recommended for the relief of any type of kidney problems, such as kidney stones, swollen kidneys, contracted kidneys, or mucus deposits in the kidneys; stomach aches, and intestinal problems such as diarrhea or constipation. Do not use for appendicitis. It can be used for stiffness in the shoulders, joints, or in other parts of the body; arthritis; rheumatism; sinus deposits, or various types of cysts or fatty-mucus deposits. For sinus problems, just dip a washcloth into the hot ginger water, wring it out, and scrub around the sinus area.

To prepare the ginger compress, grate about 3–4 tablespoons of fresh ginger root and place it on a piece of cheesecloth about 6 inches by 6 inches. Tie the cloth around the ginger to form a sack. Bring a gallon of water up to, but not over, the boiling point, reduce the flame to low and drop the sack of ginger into the water. Be careful to keep the water hot but not boiling, as boiling will destroy its effectiveness. When the water turns a milky, yellow color (after about 5 minutes), squeeze juice out of the sack into the water. Dip the middle portion of a thick cotton towel into the water by holding on to both ends, and squeeze out excess water by wringing the towel. Place hot towel directly on affected area. If the towel is too hot, shake it to allow some heat to escape. Remember, though, that the compress should be as hot as you can stand. Place a thick, dry towel over the wet towel to hold in the heat. When the towel becomes cool, remove and replace with a fresh, hot one. Repeat this for about 20 minutes. This compress stimulates blood circulation, and helps to relieve any type of tension. For the maximum effectiveness the skin should become very red.

Tofu Plaster

Tofu plasters are very good for reducing fevers, for sore throats, or for reducing swelling due to bumps on the head. Do not use for reducing fevers in case of chicken pox or measles unless the fever becomes *very* high. For measles, use a cabbage leaf on the forehead instead. Change plaster every 2–3 hours. For children it may be necessary to tie the plaster with a cloth to prevent the child from removing it.

Grind fresh *tofu* in *suribachi* and add 10%–20% whole wheat flour. Grate a small amount of ginger and add to *tofu*. Place on cheesecloth or cotton cloth, and apply to injured or affected area so that the *tofu* mixture comes in direct contact with the skin. Change plaster whenever the *tofu* grows warm.

Dentie

Dentie is a black tooth powder made from charred eggplant and sea salt. It can be bought ready-made in most natural food stores. *Dentie* is good for toothaches, gum problems, and for stopping bleeding due to cuts, nosebleeds, etc. In this case, apply directly to bleeding area. Use as a tooth powder every morning by gargling with *dentie* and then brushing. I don't recommend brushing your teeth every day with *dentie* as it is an abrasive powder and will wear down the enamel on your teeth.

You can make your own *dentie* by roasting only the top portion of the eggplant, the section closest to the stem, in the oven until it turns black. Then grind with 20%–50% sea salt into a fine powder.

Salt

Salt compresses are excellent for relieving intestinal cramps, diarrhea, menstrual cramps, or muscle stiffness.

Roast salt in dry skillet for several minutes and place inside a pillow case or cotton sack. Wrap in a towel and apply to the affected area.

Lotus-Root Tea

Lotus root is very helpful in relieving any kind of upper respiratory problems, or sinus blockage.

Grate fresh lotus root and squeeze out juice. Add an equal amount of water to juice, along with a pinch of freshly grated ginger and a pinch of sea salt. Bring to a boil, reduce flame and simmer several minutes.

If you cannot find fresh lotus root, you can substitute prepackaged, powdered losut root tea, which can be found in most natural food stores. Directions for preparation can be found on the package.

Ume-Sho-Kuzu Drink

Good for digestive disorders, especially diarrhea, and for weakness or overall lack of vitality.

Dissolve 1 heaping teaspoon of *kuzu* in a small amount of cold water and then add to 1 cup of water. Add 1 *umeboshi* plum. Bring to a boil. Reduce flame and simmer until transparent. Stir constantly to avoid lumping. Add 1 teaspoon *tamari* and serve hot.

Ume-Sho-Bancha

This easy-to-prepare beverage is good for headaches caused by the overconsumption of various types of yin foods as well as for the relief of digestive disorders.

Place 1 *umeboshi* plum (remove pit) in a cup and pour hot *bancha* tea over it. Add several drops of *tamari*, stir, and drink hot.

Daikon Tea

Daikon tea is helpful in speeding the discharge of mucus and stored animal fat, for tight kidneys or kidney stones, and for some headaches.

Grate 3 tablespoons of raw *daikon* into a cup, add a couple of drops of *tamari*. Pour hot *bancha* tea over it, and drink. If you cannot get *daikon*, use turnip or white radish. Take once a day for no more than three days at a time.

Ame-Kuzu

Ame-kuzu is very good for over-yang conditions due to the intake of excess salt.

Dissolve 1 teaspoon *kuzu* in 1 cup of water. Place in sauce pan. Add 1 table-spoon of *ame* (yinnie or rice syrup) to the *kuzu*. Turn flame to medium and slowly bring almost to a boil. Reduce flame to low and cook for 10–15 minutes. Stir constantly to avoid lumping. Serve hot.

Sesame Oil

Dark sesame oil is especially good for burns, and light sesame oil is helpful for eye problems. For eye problems, heat oil in saucepan. Strain through sterile cheesecloth or piece of cotton cloth. After it cools, store in small jar or container. Apply one or two drops to eye with an eyedropper. Strained sesame oil can also be used for ear infections.

For burns, soak the affected area in cool salt water. Then apply sesame oil.

Sesame oil is also helpful in cases where constipation has continued for over a week. Drink 1 or 2 tablespoons of raw sesame oil for several days.

Sesame oil can also be used as a hand lotion for chapped, sore, and red skin.

Shiitake Mushroom Tea

Good for helping the body discharge excess yang such as animal food, fish, buckwheat, salt.

Boil 2–3 *shiitake* in water. Remove *shiitake* and drink liquid. Drink only 1 small cup as it is very strong. Wait several days before drinking again.

Rice Bran Compress

Make a thick paste of water and rice bran and apply to affected area. Change compress as it becomes warm. It will draw out the heat from the affected area.

This is especially good for frostbite or fevers in specific areas of the limbs. Never place a frostbitten area in hot or warm water. Instead place in cool water for several minutes, then apply rice bran compress.

For a more complete list of medicinal home preparations, please see *Natural Healing through Macrobiotics* by Michio Kushi, published by Japan Publications, Inc.

Menu

These menus are only basic suggestions for planning daily meals. Your menus should vary from week to week as well as seasonally, allowing for changes in the weather and in your activity and condition.

Monday

Breakfast	**Lunch**	**Dinner**
Soft rice	Fried rice	Brown rice
Miso soup	Vegetables	Millet soup
Bancha tea	*Bancha* tea	*Azuki* beans
		Steamed cauliflower and broccoli
		Oatmeal cookies
		Bancha tea

Tuesday

Breakfast	**Lunch**	**Dinner**
Soft millet	Whole wheat noodles	Brown rice
Miso soup	Broccoli	Onion soup
Bancha tea	*Bancha* tea	Baked squash
		Arame
		Watercress
		Bancha tea

Wednesday

Breakfast	**Lunch**	**Dinner**
Oatmeal	Rice ball	Brown rice
Miso soup	Sautéed cabbage	Squash soup
Bancha tea	*Bancha* tea	Boiled salad with *tofu* dressing
		Baked carrots, onions and *kombu*
		Kanten
		Bancha tea

Thursday

Breakfast
Soft rice with squash
Miso soup
Bancha tea

Lunch
Soba and broth
Bancha tea

Dinner
Brown rice
Barley *seitan* soup
Boiled *daikon*
Sautéed cabbage and corn
Bancha tea

Friday

Breakfast
Oatmeal
Miso soup
Bancha tea

Lunch
Steamed bread
Boiled vegetables
Bancha tea

Dinner
Brown rice
Tamari broth soup with
    watercress
Kidney beans
Wakame and onions
Boiled carrots
Apple strudel
Bancha tea

Saturday

Breakfast
Soft rice with
    Chinese cabbage
Miso soup
Bancha tea

Lunch
Rice ball
Vegetables
Bancha tea

Dinner
Brown rice
Millet with vegetables
Black bean soup
Swiss chard
Sautéed cauliflower
Bancha tea

Sundy

Breakfast
Oatmeal with onions
Miso soup
Bancha tea

Lunch
Fried rice or noodles
Steamed vegetables
Bancha tea

Dinner
Brown rice
Corn soup
Seitan croquettes
Kale
Kombu with onions and carrots
Apple pie
Bancha tea

Standard Suggestions for the Macrobiotic Diet and Way of Life*

General Way of Life

1. Let us live happily without being preoccupied about our health, and let us be active both mentally and physically.
2. Let us be grateful for everything and for everyone, and let us pray before and after each meal.
3. Please retire before midnight whenever possible, and get up early in the morning.
4. Please avoid wearing any synthetic or woolen clothing directly in contact with the body, and please avoid using excessive metallic accessories on the fingers, wrists or neck, keeping such ornaments as simple and graceful as possible.
5. Please chew very well, at least 50 times for each mouthful.
6. If your strength permits, please go outdoors often, in simple clothing, if possible, barefoot. Walk on the grass and soil up to one half-hour, every fine day.
7. Please keep your home in good order, from the kitchen, bathroom, bedroom and living rooms, to every corner of the house.
8. Initiate and maintain an active correspondence, extending your love and friendship towards parents, brothers and sisters, relatives, teachers, and friends.
9. Avoid taking long baths or showers unless you have been consuming too much salt or animal food.
10. Rub down your whole body with either a hot damp towel or a dry towel until the skin becomes red, every morning or every night before retiring. If that is not possible, at least do the hands and feet, each finger and toe.
11. Please avoid using chemically perfumed cosmetics. For care of the teeth, use natural preparations or sea salt to brush every morning and night.
12. If your physical condition allows, please do vigorous exercise regularly, including scrubbing floors, cleaning windows, washing clothes; if desired you may participate in systemic forms of exercise such as yoga, martial arts or sports.

---

* Adapted with permission from the teachings of Michio Kushi.

Standard Dietary Recommendations

1. At least 50% by volume cooked of every meal should be whole cereal grains, prepared with a variety of cooking methods. Whole cereal grains include brown rice, whole wheat, whole wheat bread, whole wheat chapatis, whole wheat noodles, barley, millet, oats, oatmeal, corn, corn on the cob, corn grits, buckwheat groats, buckwheat noodles, rye, rye bread, etc.

2. Approximately 5% of daily food intake by volume should include *miso* soup or *tamari* broth soup (one or two small bowls). The taste should not be too salty. The ingredients should include various vegetables, seaweeds, beans and grains; alter the recipe often.

3. About 20% to 30% of each meal may include vegetables: 2/3 of them cooked in various styles, including sautéing, steaming, boiling, baking; up to 1/3 of them as raw salad. Mayonnaise and commercial dressings should be avoided. Potatoes, including sweet potatoes and yams, tomatoes, eggplants, asparagus, spinach, beets, zucchini squash, avocado and any other tropical vegetables should be avoided, unless you live in a tropical region.

4. From 10% to 15% of daily intake should include cooked beans and seaweed. Beans for daily use are *azuki* beans, chickpeas, lentils, black beans. Other beans are for occasional use only. Seaweeds such as *hijiki*, *kombu*, *wakame*, *nori*, dulse, agar-agar, and Irish moss can be prepared with a variety of cooking methods. These dishes should be flavored with a moderate amount of *tamari* soy sauce or sea salt.

5. Once or twice a week, a small volume of white-meat fish may be eaten. The method of cooking should vary every week. A fruit dessert may also be eaten two or three times a week, provided the fruits grow in the local climatic zone. Thus, if you live in a temperate zone, avoid tropical and semi-tropical fruits. Fruit juice is not advisable, although occasional consumption in very hot weather may be moderately indulged. Roasted seeds and roasted nuts, with a slight salt taste, may be enjoyed as a snack or supplement as well as dried fruits and roasted beans.

6. Beverages recommended include *bancha* twig tea (roasted), *Mu* tea, dandelion tea, cereal grain coffee or tea, all for daily use, as well as any traditional tea which does not have an aromatic fragrance and a stimulant effect.

7. Foods which may need to be reduced or avoided in a temperate climate:
   —Meat, animal fat, poultry, dairy food, butter.
   —Tropical and semi-tropical fruits and fruit juice; soda, artificial drinks and beverages; coffee, colored tea, and all aromatic stimulant teas such as mint or peppermint tea.
   —Sugar, honey, all syrups, saccharine and other artificial sweeteners (rice honey or barley malt may be used in very small quantities occasionally to add a sweet taste if necessary).

—Hot spices, any aromatic, stimulant food, food accessories, and artificial beverages; also artificial vinegar.

8. Additional suggestions:
    —Cooking oil should be of vegetable origin; if you wish to improve your health, limit oil to good quality sesame oil and corn oil, in moderate volume.
    —Salt should be unrefined sea salt. *Tamari* soy sauce and *miso*, prepared in the traditional way, may be used as salty seasoning.
    —The following condiments are recommended:
     1. *Gomasio* (10 to 12 parts roasted sesame seeds, to 1 part sea salt)
     2. Roasted kelp powder, roasted *wakame* powder
     3. *Umeboshi* plums
     4. *Tekka*
     5. *Tamari* soy sauce (moderate use, only for mild taste)

    You may eat 2–3 times per day regularly, as much as you want, provided the proportion is correct and chewing is thorough. Please avoid eating for approximately 3 hours before sleeping. For thirst, you may drink a small amount of water, but not iced.

9. Final advice: Proper cooking is so important that everyone is advised to learn the way of cooking by attending cooking classes or through the advice from experienced senior friends, and also trying out recipes in macrobiotic cook books.

Principles of the Order of the Universe

Seven Universal Principles of the Infinite Universe

1. Everything is a differentiation of one Infinity.
2. Everything changes.
3. All antagonisms are complementary.
4. There is nothing identical.
5. What has a front has a back.
6. The bigger the front, the bigger the back.
7. What has a beginning has an end.

Twelve Laws of Change of the Infinite Universe

1. One Infinity manifests itself into complementary and antagonistic tendencies, yin and yang, in its endless change.
2. Yin and yang are manifested continuously from the eternal movement of one infinite universe.
3. Yin represents centrifugality. Yang represents centripetality. Yin and yang together produce energy and all phenomena.
4. Yin attracts yang. Yang attracts yin.
5. Yin repels yin. Yang repels yang.
6. Yin and yang combined in varying proportions produce different phenomena. The attraction and repulsion among phenomena is proportional to the difference of the yin and yang forces.
7. All phenomena are ephemeral, constantly changing their constitution of yin and yang forces; yin changes into yang, yang changes into yin.
8. Nothing is solely yin or solely yang. Everything is composed of both tendencies in varying degrees.
9. There is nothing neuter. Either yin or yang is in excess in every occurrence.
10. Large yin attracts small yin. Large yang attracts small yang.
11. Extreme yin produces yang, and extreme yang produces yin.
12. All physical manifestations are yang at the center, and yin at the surface.

Classification of Yin and Yang

Characteristic	YIN (▽) Centrifugal Force	YANG (△) Centripetal Force
Tendency	Expansion	Contraction
Function	Diffusion	Fusion
	Dispersion	Assimilation
	Separation	Gathering
	Decomposition	Organization
Movement	More inactive and slower	More active and faster
Vibration	Shorter wave and higher frequency	Longer wave and lower frequency
Direction	Ascent and vertical	Descent and horizontal
Position	More outward and periphery	More inward and central
Weight	Lighter	Heavier
Temperature	Colder	Hotter
Light	Darker	Brighter
Humidity	More wet	More dry
Density	Thinner	Thicker
Size	Longer	Smaller
Shape	More expansive and fragile	More contractive and harder
Form	Longer	Shorter
Texture	Softer	Harder
Atomic particle	Electron	Proton
Elements	N, O, K, P, Ca, etc.	H, C, Na, As, Mg, etc.
Environment	Vibration .... Air .... Water .... Earth	
Climatic effects	Tropical climate	Colder climate
Biological	More vegetable quality	More animal quality
Sex	Female	Male
Organ structure	More hollow and expansive	More compacted and condensed
Nerves	More peripheral, orthosympathetic	More central, parasympathetic
Attitude	More gentle, negative	More active, positive
Work	More psychological and mental	More physical and social
Dimension	Space	Time

Glossary

agar-agar A white gelatin derived from a species of seaweed. Used in making *kanten* and aspics.

ai knife A Japanese vegetable knife with a pointed tip.

ame A natural grain sweetener made from either rice, barley or wheat, or a combination of grains. Frequently called rice honey or yinnie syrup.

amasake A sweetener or refreshing drink made from fermented sweet rice.

arrowroot A starch flour processed from the root of a native American plant. It is used as a thickening agent, similar to cornstarch or *kuzu*, for making sauces, stews, gravies or desserts.

azuki beans A small, dark red bean imported from Japan, but also grown in this country. Especially good for the kidneys.

bancha tea Correctly named *Kukicha*, *bancha* consists of the stems and leaves from tea bushes that are at least three years old. It is grown in Japan. *Bancha* tea aids in digestion and is high in calcium. It contains no chemical dyes or caffeine. *Bancha* makes an excellent after-dinner beverage.

bonito flakes Fish flakes shaved from dried bonito fish. Used in soup stocks or as a garnish for soups and noodle dishes.

brown rice miso A fermented soybean paste made from brown rice, soybeans and sea salt.

burdock A wild, hardy plant that grows throughout most of the United States. The long, dark root is highly valued in macrobiotic cooking for its strengthening qualities. The Japanese name is *Gobo*.

chirimen iriko Very small dried fish. High in iron and calcium.

daikon A long, white radish. Besides making a delicious side dish, *daikon* is a specific for cutting fat and mucus deposits that have accumulated in our bodies as a result of past animal food intake. Grated *daikon* aids in the digestion of oily foods.

dentie A black tooth powder made from sea salt and charred eggplant.

dulse A reddish-purple seaweed. Used in soups, salads, and vegetable dishes. Very high in iron.

Foley food mill A special steel food mill, which is operated by a hand crank to make purées, sauces, dips, etc.

ganmodoki A deep-fried cake made from *tofu* and a variety of different vegetables.

ginger A spicy, pungent, golden-colored root, used in cooking and for medicinal purposes.

ginger compress Sometimes called a ginger fomentation. A compress made from grated ginger root and water. Applied hot to an affected area of the body, it will stimulate circulation and dissolve stagnation.

gluten The sticky substance that remains after the bran has been kneaded and rinsed from flour. Used to make *seitan* and *fu*.

gomasio A condiment made from roasted, ground sesame seeds and sea salt.

Hatcho miso A soybean paste made from soybeans and sea salt and aged for at least 3 years. Used in making condiments, soup stocks, seasoning for vegetable dishes, etc.

hijiki A dark brown seaweed which, when dried, turns black. It is strong and wiry. Hijiki is native to Japan but also grows off the coast of Maine.

Hokkaido pumpkin A round, dark green or orange squash, which is very sweet. It is harvested in early fall. Originated in New England and was introduced to Japan and named after the island of Hokkaido.

jinenjo	A light brown Japanese mountain potato which grows to be several feet long and two to three inches wide.
kanten	A jelled dessert made from fruit and agar-agar.
kasha knishes	Cakes made from buckwheat and vegetables, wrapped in a pastry dough and baked.
kasha varnitchkes	Fried buckwheat, noodles, and vegetables.
kayu	Long-cooked grain prepared with approximately five times as much water as grain. *Kayu* is ready when it is very soft and creamy.
kinpira	A sautéed burdock or burdock and carrot dish, which is seasoned with *tamari*.
koji	Grain that has been innoculated with the same type of bacteria that is used in making such fermented foods and drinks as *miso*, *tamari*, *amasake* and *sake*.
kombu	A wide, thick, dark green seaweed which grows in deep ocean water. Used in making soup stocks, cooked with vegetables, in soups, condiments, candy, etc.
kombu dashi	A soup broth made from *kombu* and water.
kome miso	Rice *miso*. Usually white rice *miso*, made from white rice, soybeans and sea salt.
kukicha	Usually called *bancha*. Older stems and leaves of a tea bush grown in Japan.
kuzu	A white starch made from the root of the wild *kuzu* plant. In this country the plant is called "kudzu." Used in making soups, sauces, gravies, desserts, and for medicinal purposes.
layering method	A method of cooking soups, vegetables, beans, grains, etc., in which ingredients are layered in ascending order in the cooking pot from yin to yang.
lotus root	The root of a variety of water lily which is brown-skinned with a hollow, chambered, off-white inside. Especially good for respiratory organs.
mekabu	Roots of the *wakame* seaweed plant. Used in making soups and soup stocks. Has a very strong flavor.
mochi	A rice cake or dumpling made from cooked, pounded sweet rice.
mugicha	A tea made out of roasted, unhulled barley and water.
mugi miso	Soybean paste made from barley, soybeans, sea salt and water.
mugwort	A wild plant which can be dried and made into tea, or pounded with sweet rice to make mugwort *mochi*. Has medicinal properties.
mu tea	A tea made from 16 different herbs. It is very yang and has certain medicinal values.
natto	Soybeans which have been cooked and mixed with beneficial enzymes and allowed to ferment for 24 hours under a controlled temperature.
natto miso	A condiment *miso*, which is not actually *natto*. It is made from soybeans, grain, ginger and *kombu*, and fermented for a very short time.
nigari	Hard, crystallized salt made from the liquid drippings of dampened sea salt. Used in making *tofu*.
nori	Thin sheets of dried seaweed. Black or dark purple when dried. Roasted over a flame until green. Used as a garnish, wrapped around rice balls, in making *sushi*, or cooked with *tamari* and used as a condiment.
ohagi	A rice cake made from cooked, pounded sweet rice and coated with items such as *azuki* beans, chestnuts, roasted, chopped, ground nuts, sesame seeds, soybean flour, etc.
okara	The coarse soybean pulp left over when making *tofu*. Cooked with vegetables.
sashimi	Raw, sliced fish.
sea salt	Salt obtained from the ocean as opposed to land salt. It is either sun baked or kiln baked. High in trace minerals, it contains no chemicals, sugar, or iodine.
seitan	Wheat gluten cooked in *tamari*, *kombu* and water.
shio kombu	Pieces of *kombu* cooked for a long time in *tamari* and used in small amounts as a condiment.
shiitake	A medicinal, dried mushroom imported from Japan.
soba	Noodles made from buckwheat flour or a combination of buckwheat flour with whole wheat flour or *jinenjo* flour.

sukiyaki	A one-dish meal prepared in a large cast iron skillet, containing a variety of vegetables, noodles, seaweeds, *seitan*, *tofu*, fish, etc.
suribachi	A special serrated, glazed clay bowl. Used with a pestle (called a *surikoji*) for grinding and puréeing foods.
sushi	Rice rolled with vegetables, fish, or pickles, wrapped in *nori* and sliced into rounds.
sushi mat	A mat made from strips of bamboo tied together with string. Used in making *sushi*, or as a cover for bowls.
takuan	*Daikon* which is pickled in rice bran and sea salt. Sometimes spelled "takuwan."
taro	A potato which has a thick, hairy skin. Often called *albi*. Used in making *taro* or *albi* plasters to draw toxins from the body, or can be eaten as a vegetable.
tamari	Name given to traditional, naturally made soy sauce to distinguish it from the commercial, chemically processed variety.
tekka	Condiment made from *Hatcho* miso, sesame oil, burdock, lotus root, carrot, and ginger root. Sautéed on a low flame for several hours.
tempeh	A dish made from split soybeans, vinegar, water and a special bacteria, which is allowed to ferment for several hours. Eaten in Indonesia and Ceylon as a staple food. Available prepacked, ready to make, in some natural food stores.
tempura	Sliced vegetables, fish, or patties made of grain, vegetables, fish *tofu*, etc., which are dipped into a batter and deep fried until golden brown.
tofu	A cake made from soybeans, *nigari*, and water.
umeboshi	A salty pickled plum.
wakame	A long, thin, green seaweed used in making soups, salads, vegetable dishes, etc.
yannoh	A grain coffee made from five different grains and beans which have been roasted and ground into a fine powder.
yuba	Dried soy milk.

Index